To: Roger Matthews,
Your dedication and years of service to this movement has touched so many lives!
Steve Mundahl
9/30/02

100 YEARS OF
Goodwill

Touching Lives Through the Power of Work

Steve Mundahl

Foreword by Evelyne Villines

i

Published by
Circe Press
(Publishers of Lifestyles Press)
P.O. Box 493
Greensboro, NC 27402
888-742-2155

ISBN #1-58320-050-9

Cover design by The Gemini Group
Edited by Henri Forget

Photos courtesy of:
Goodwill Industries International
Goodwill Industries of Central North Carolina, Inc.
Morgan Memorial Goodwill Industries, Inc.

Goodwill cover logo courtesy of
Goodwill Industries International

Preface

As an employee of Goodwill Industries, I am not sure who is most served, those whom we train, or those of us who are employed to serve this special group of individuals.

During 2002 Goodwill Industries celebrates its rich centennial history of serving individuals with disabilities and disadvantages. Goodwill was founded on the principle that through work, not charity, self-sufficiency can ultimately be attained. Converting society's discarded clothing and household goods into a worldwide network of agencies, Goodwill Industries has served almost six million individuals during its first 100 years.

The profiles that follow are of ordinary individuals, all of whom have lived extraordinary lives. Through my experience with Goodwill, I have discovered the great hearts of so many people who have entered Goodwill training programs or who are employed by Goodwill. There appears to be a common thread among these quiet, hard-working individuals, many of whom are truly remarkable. Whatever they seem to lack because of their disability, they make up for it with heart and determination. It is my hope this book will add value and credence to their struggles.

Steve Mundahl, June 2002

Dedicated to
Theresa, Bernadette, Ed, Debbie, Cynthia,
Charles, Karan and so many others who
have shown us all what size our
hearts really should to be.

Special thanks to
Richard J. Gorham, President/CEO, Goodwill
Industries of Central North Carolina, Inc. for his
support and friendship.

Foreword
Evelyne Jobe Villines

*To live, is the rarest thing in the world; most people
exist, that is all.*
Oscar Wilde.

Through my years as an advocate for persons
who are disabled, I have come to know most of
the worldwide leadership of Goodwill Industries.
My respect for the dedication of these leaders of
Goodwill and the quiet work that they do every
day in cities and villages all over the world is
boundless.

Having been appointed by a president of the
United States to work to provide services to
persons who are blind or severely disabled and
having worked with individuals who are disabled
for most of my life in various capacities, I was
pleased to be asked to be involved in the writing
of this book. While many organizations provide
services to persons who are disabled, few have
done such an admirable job, or for as long, as
Goodwill Industries.

Recycling waste of households throughout the
world is hardly glamorous work. Assisting adults
who are disabled and/or disadvantaged every day
to learn good work habits and develop valuable
work skills so they might also realize the "good
life" dream is work that is difficult, yet vital to
those who need it most. Living a self-sufficient life
can be a difficult proposition for those who are
disabled. It might only be a distant dream for
someone with a severe physical disability, or for

an individual who is blind or hearing impaired. Often the economic models of companies throughout the world do not include employees who have such disabilities.

Gathering the immense volume of unwanted articles of clothing, furniture, appliances and housewares and converting those discarded products into a $1.4 billion industry serving the employment needs of millions of persons who are disabled and/or disadvantaged and their families is nothing short of astounding, yet immensely hard work. I have had the honor and pleasure of meeting some of the army of Goodwill employees who assist mothers on welfare, and individuals severely disabled in communities across America and the world. In my travels I see their faces, experience their dedication and commitment, and marvel at their patience. Were it not for a few special individuals in my life who displayed that same patience and dedication, I may have experienced a very different type of life.

Oscar Wilde said: "To live, is the rarest thing in the world; most people exist, that is all." His words are so poignant. At the age of three, while playing in the yard of my Iowa home, my legs suddenly would not allow me to stand. Two days later our family physician referred me to a specialist from Omaha who said I would not live through the night. The diagnosis was infantile paralysis, now known as polio. Needless to say, I made it through the night.

Two years later I started school and when the teacher saw me on crutches, she commented, "I don't have time to teach a handicapped child," and I was sent home. I had never heard the word before and didn't know what a "handicap" was. I asked my mother later that afternoon, "Am I a handicapped child?" Luckily for me my father was the mayor of that small Iowa town and my uncle was a member of the school board and the way was paved for me to attend school, even with my "handicap."

The truth was, and is in far too many places still, that an individual who is disabled is not considered a "whole" person. Our society is geared to persons who are the tallest, strongest, prettiest, slenderest, and the fastest, not persons who are disabled or disadvantaged. As a child, I longed to be like other kids: to run, play tag, dribble a basketball, and ride a bicycle. Instead, I was often given pity, extra study periods or just ignored, which really hurt me.

Because of my disability, I was not welcome in the school system. I simply didn't fit in. It seemed most in society didn't care to view anyone with a disability, whether it was mental, physical, emotional or financial. At the age of nine my parents took me to a crippled children's hospital 250 miles away so that I could receive corrective surgery and rehabilitative care. I lived there most of the time until I was sixteen. I was a patient on Ward D, which I came to know as an initial for "Devil." The dehumanization that took place in that hospital created nightmares that existed in my life for years to come. Although I was scrubbed down with lye soap every day so that I was always clean, I never felt more unclean. As a young teenage girl, I just wanted to be normal, to fit in. I wanted to play basketball and go on dates. I wanted to dance with the other kids and be a cheerleader.

While at the crippled children's hospital, I received a series of operations, including one that placed my legs in a cast with a thirty-six-inch rod between my ankles. My left hip was operated on as was my right knee. The physical pain I felt was excruciating, but the emotional pain of "being different" and homesick was worse. On occasional trips home, I would go back to school where I just wanted to "fit in."

What I didn't realize then, however, was that I was someone very special. My disability made me a stronger person. While I was forced to live a different life, I also received different blessings. I grew up with an inner resolve I didn't even know I possessed until I was older. I see that same resolve, those same problems in children and adults who are disabled wherever I travel, and I count my blessings everyday.

I left the crippled children's hospital when I was sixteen. Later I married and it seemed a miracle when I became pregnant because eight doctors had told me I could never have children. The night they laid my first baby in my arms I felt "whole." It is love that makes us whole. I have three wonderful children, Christine, Julia and Wesley. Because Goodwill Industries was founded on love and continues to assist people with disabilities to become whole.

For persons with a disability, life isn't quite the same as for those who constantly misjudge and misunderstand us. We must cope with our disability. Wherever I travel and to whomever I speak, I often wish that they could see life through my eyes, and realize that being born with, acquiring a disability, or being in a disadvantaged position in life, doesn't make us different or less worthy of a good job and a full life. For every individual or company that discriminates against persons who are visually impaired or mentally retarded, because these individuals don't appear "whole," the disability squarely belongs to the discriminator, not to us.

As a person who travels often and sometimes utilizes a wheelchair, there have been attempts to "put me in the corner" and to be ignored. It is not unusual to have to request assistance to board a plane or get a cab. Often in public places, it is the person who pushes the wheelchair that is spoken to, not the person in the chair. I no longer remain silent. I have learned to be quite vocal.

The efforts of a single man over one hundred years ago to bring needed services and attention to the population of persons who are disabled or disadvantaged throughout the world have transformed the lives of millions of people. Five million individuals have already been assisted in the one hundred years of Goodwill. At the dawn of the second one hundred years of Goodwill, the leadership of this movement has set a lofty goal – to serve twenty million people in the next eighteen years, by 2020. In the true spirit of Goodwill's founder, Edgar Helms, Goodwill's mission of offering a hand up, not a hand out has been a quietly working force that is transforming millions of lives. Also in Helm's own words, "There is much work yet to do."

To employers, I offer this message: Persons with disabilities have wonderful abilities and talents to offer your company. Please look beyond the eyes that do not see, or the body that cannot walk. Please look past the mental challenge that may be obvious and take note of the heart of that person – it is a heart that loves easily because it has known its share of hurt.

To persons with disabilities I would encourage you to share your disability. Don't hide behind physical or mental problems. They have helped make you strong. Ask for that special job and reassure your employer that "you can do" the job. Never forget that you are a part of the same fabric of society as anyone else, and you have much to contribute. You are needed, loved and wanted.

To the employees and leadership of Goodwill, and all the other agencies who work with this special population of individuals, never forget the words of Edgar Helms: "Be dissatisfied with your work until every handicapped and unfortunate person in your community has an opportunity to develop to his/her fullest usefulness and enjoy a maximum of abundant living." Employees and leaders of agencies who serve those with barriers to employment are doing important work. With seven out of ten persons with disabilities experiencing unemployment we have far to go and much work to do. Become a vocal advocate and a strong voice for those who need your words of encouragement, education and enlightenment.

Finally, to the readers of this book: Take time to visit a Goodwill agency in your community. You may contribute a bag of clothing, small wares, books or furniture, but until you see the work of Goodwill up close, you might miss the real magic of transformation that occurs every day at over two hundred Goodwill agencies throughout the world. Remember also that those with a disability or who have become America's disadvantaged want the same opportunities that you do – a good, productive and abundant life.

After a career with Easter Seals, the Iowa state government and as a volunteer for over thirty years with Goodwill Industries, it has been a privilege and honor to work with the many agencies across the country and throughout the world in serving persons experiencing barriers to employment. To be a part of the centennial story of Goodwill is also a privilege.

NISH, the "National Industries for the Severely Handicapped" named their outstanding Graduate of the Year award in honor of Evelyne Villines. The Evelyne R. Villines Graduate of the Year Award recognizes outstanding disabled achievers from all walks of life. Ms. Villines is a sought after public speaker and advocate for all persons with disabilities. To request Ms. Villines appearance at your company or function, contact the publisher.

Adult Onset Bipolar Disorder
A Life Changing Event...

...Karan's Story

Bipolar disorder, also known as manic-depressive illness, is a brain disorder that causes unusual shifts in a person's mood, energy and their ability to function normally. The National Mental Health Association estimates that one to two percent of the population, over two million American adults, suffer from bipolar disorder.

The symptoms of bipolar disorder are severe. Cycles of mania (manic) in which the individual is "up" or hyper, are followed by deep cycles of depression, to the point the individual can be suicidal. Both cycles are often so disruptive that relationships can be damaged, job and school performance can easily suffer, all of which can bring the patient to the brink of suicide. The disorder distorts moods, thoughts and emotion and destroys the foundation of rationale thought and behavior. It also erodes the will and desire to live.

There are three major levels of bipolar disorders. The degree or severity of the mania and depression cycles differentiates them, and whichever predominates in the individual's behavior. These dramatic mood swings, from overly "high" and/or irritable to sad and hopeless, and then back again, are often filled with periods of normal moods. The highs and lows of these cycles are called episodes. Episodes can be psychotic where hallucinations, voices and delusions are present.

While both sexes are equally prone to the disease, unlike depression, alone which is predominant in women, there are differences in the course and treatment of the disease. Women are more likely to rapidly cycle between high and low moods. Women with bipolar disorders are also at a higher risk of relapse in the postpartum period.

Although there is no known cure for the disease, bipolar disorder can be treated effectively, resulting in a near normal life for the individual. While a cure eludes mental health professionals, there is a known genetic predisposition to bipolar disorder. This disorder seems to run in families, a gene that is passed from parent to child. While there is a genetic basis to bipolar, it is believed that genetics do not always apply, with the disease skipping generations, even siblings.

Treatment varies from individual to individual, but usually involves medication and psychological treatment (talk therapy) for successful management of the disease. Medications are typically "mood stabilizers." Often this medication will be prescribed for years, even for the duration of the patient's life.

Because of the devastating cycles of depression and mania that accompany bipolar disorder, alcohol and drug abuse are very common among people with the disease. Anxiety disorders, such as obsessive-compulsive disorder and post-traumatic stress disorder are also common in people with bipolar disorder.

The National Institute of Mental Health (NIMH) is currently researching new treatment methods for bipolar disorder. A new program recently introduced by NIMH is called The Systematic Treatment Enhancement Program for Bipolar Disorder (STEP-BD).

To learn more about recently introduced treatment programs, as well as general information about bipolar disorder, you may wish to write or visit any of the following agencies for assistance:

- National Institute of Mental Health (NIMH)
  6001 Executive Bvld., Bethesda, MD 20892
  301-443-4513; website at: www.nimh.nih.gov.

- Child & Adolescent Bipolar Foundation
  1187 Willmette Avenue, PMB #331,Willmette,
  IL. 60091; 847-256-8525; website at:
  www.bpkids.org

- Depression & Related Affective Disorders

Johns Hopkins Hospital, Meyer 3-181; 600 North Wolfe Street, Baltimore, MD 21287; 410-955-4647

website at: www.med.jhu.edu/drada

- National Alliance for the Mentally Ill (NAMI) Colonial Place Three, 2107 Wilson Blvd., Arlington, VA 22201; 800-950-6264; website at: www.nami.org

- National Depressive and Manic-Depressive 730 N. Franklin Street, Suite 501, Chicago, IL. 60610, 800-826-3632 website at: www.ndmda.org

- National Foundation for Depressive Illness, Inc., P.O. Box 2257, New York, NY 10116; 800-239-1265 website at: www.depression.org

- National Mental Health Assn. 1021 Prince Street, Alexandria, VA 22314 800-969-6642; website at: www.nmha.org

Karan's Story
A Life Changing Event...

...Adult Onset Bipolar Disorder

For most of us, mental illness is a disorder that "other" people have. In an American culture that emphasizes beauty, athleticism, superior intelligence, success and, personal liberties, mental illness epitomizes just the opposite. Once diagnosed with mental illness, friends and family are quick to desert you – just as the cultural landscape of the American workplace recedes before you. The result often forces an individual to keep their illness in secret and shame, if they can.

Karan was in the prime of her career when she was diagnosed with adult onset, bipolar disorder. She understands all too well that a battle with the disorder is often the easiest obstacle to overcome. It is the mountain of public perception and prejudice that often leaves the victim of mental illness alone at the bottom and ill equipped to put their life back together.

Karan lived and worked in a small community in Kentucky, and had worked at the same job for the past five years. She held a responsible job that she had worked very hard to obtain. She had recently been promoted at the age of twenty-eight, and now supervised a large staff. It had been the fulfillment of a personal goal and she had been working many long hours to make it happen. Working triple shifts, Karan often worked twenty-three hours at a time before allowing herself to rest for a few hours and returning to work.

It was following a few hours of sleep that Karan awoke, ate a light breakfast and drove herself to work one morning. While this fall morning had started out being no different than any other, it would be a morning that would change her life forever.

"I was driving to work on that morning and all of a sudden just blanked out. I didn't know who I was or where I was going. One moment I was driving up to a stop sign with thoughts of the day on my mind and the next moment I couldn't remember what my name was."

As she looked up, Karan saw nothing that she recognized. Every building, every house, even the name of the street she was on was unknown to her. Fighting off a sudden panic attack, Karan drove through the light and pulled into a convenience store parking lot, bringing her car to a stop.

"I looked down and saw that I was wearing a white uniform with a name badge on it. I took off the name badge and read a name that I didn't even recognize... K-a-r-a-n H-a-y-e-s. Feeling very frightened and very panicky I took hold of the steering wheel, drawing a deep breath and concentrated with all of my might to remember what I had been just doing and where I was going."

Karan was a total stranger to the person in the car that morning. She looked into the car's mirror for some sign of recognition, but the blank stare of a total stranger looked back at her.

"I sat for a while trying to make sense of this. I read the name badge again and started checking my uniform pockets for some idea of where I was going and who I was, but I found nothing that gave me a clue. I looked through my purse, opening my billfold.

I found my driver's license and the face and address on it also drew a blank."

She put the billfold back in her purse, took a deep breath and got of her car and walked into the convenience store. Although consumed with panic inside, Karan managed a smile, trying not to draw attention to how she felt.

"Excuse me, sir, I'm new in town, ready to start a new job and was given this name badge, but I don't know how to get to this place on the badge. Can you give me some directions?"

Her thoughts were that if she could somehow get to the place that was named on the I.D. badge on her uniform, perhaps she could sort out this total lack of cognitive memory or at least get some help once she got there. She thought of turning around, but had no idea where she had just come from. Fighting to remain calm she waited for the gas station attendant to answer her. He was looking at her with the oddest stare, making Karan feel even more uncomfortable.

"He finally answered me and said, 'If you buy a Pepsi from me, I'll tell you how to get there.' I just stared back at him, thinking to myself, what an odd thing to say. But I went to the cooler, picked out a soft drink, paid for it and waited for his directions, which he finally gave to me."

Unbeknown to her that morning, Karan regularly stopped at that convenience store every morning for a Pepsi on her way to work. The attendant had recognized her and thought that she was playing a joke with him at first, but seeing the faraway look on her face that morning, the attendant deduced that there might be something wrong with her and gave her easy-to-follow, turn-by-turn directions to her place of employment.

"I got back into my car and literally was just holding myself together by this point. I was frozen with fear and was trembling so hard I could hardly get the keys into the ignition. I followed the man's instructions and in a few minutes drove into the parking lot of the nursing home. I took a deep breath and prayed that somehow I would know this place and wake up from this dream state I was in. As I got out the car, a ring of keys fell out of my uniform pocket onto the ground. The facility's name, matching my name tag was on the key ring."

Karan deduced that she must be somebody important to this facility or she wouldn't have so many keys. Dozens of keys were on the ring, and although she couldn't recognize a single key, she knew that she must be someone of great responsibility. A flicker of hope stemmed the rising panic. She gathered what strength remained in her and left her car, walking confidently toward the front door. She took a deep breath and entered. Immediately the usual morning salutations from fellow employees began.

"Good morning, Karan."

"Morning, Ms. Hayes."

"Hi Karan, get some sleep?"

9

Karan answered each greeting with her own, smiling confidently, but not recognizing a single face.

"I walked down one hall and looked into the rooms and immediately saw that it was a health care facility of some sort. I walked down the end of a second hall and saw a reality orientation board that had the date of June 24, 1984. The board also gave the weather as being cloudy with the possibility of rain. I looked at the board and at least knew that this day was June 24, 1984. Prior to seeing that board I wouldn't have been able to even the guess the year, much less the month or the day. I looked at the name of the center on the board and read it out loud: BOWLING GREEN HEALTH CARE CENTER."

Not knowing where to go, Karan headed down a third corridor and as she came to the end of the hall, she looked up at a closed door that said, KARAN HAYES, DIRECTOR OF NURSING.

"My response was, oh shit. My only thought was that I had to get into the office before I started screaming and succumbing to the rising panic that I felt. I fumbled for the large set of keys in my pocket but not knowing which key fit the lock to my office, I grew more and more panicky with each key I tried."

A healthcare technician saw Karan struggling with the keys and offered her assistance. She accepted, making up an excuse that she wasn't feeling well and needed help to get inside her office. Immediately the technician opened the door for her and Karan went in, closing the door, almost slamming it behind her. Karan locked the office door, took the phone off the hook, closed the curtains to the windows and started to cry.

The healthcare attendant went to the administrator of the facility after she noticed Karan's odd behavior. Ms. Hayes had never closed the door, much less locked it in the past, and was a lover of sunlight, so the attendant found it odd that the director of nursing would close all of the blinds and not answer the phone or knocks of concern at her door.

Bernice, the administrator, was a close friend of Karan's and took her master key, entered the office and found Karan sobbing uncontrollably at her desk. Karan looked up at her administrator and recognized her as Bernice. The two women talked for awhile and Karan felt better at least for recognizing someone. She told the administrator of the extraordinary events of the morning and hugged the older woman as though her life depended on it.

Bernice asked Karan if she remembered a woman named Christine. When Karan shook her head no, Bernice told Karan that Christine was a psychologist that Karan had been seeing for a week about depression.

The psychologist was called and the immediate thought was that Karan had a brain tumor or similar disorder, causing sudden onset of memory loss. A psychiatrist was consulted and Karan was admitted to the hospital's psychiatric ward. By noon, Karan had been hospitalized and a battery of tests was given to her. After eight days, all tests had returned negative. Hospital staff members were perplexed. The admitting psychiatrist spoke with Karan and told her that he was going to administer one last examination. Although she appeared too young for any hope of positive response to the test, he needed an explanation for her memory loss. The test was called the DES, a genetic examination for bipolar disorder. Adult onset bipolar disorder usually occurs in a person's forties or fifties, and although she was only twenty-eight, the test came back positive for Karan.

When the admitting psychiatrist spoke with Karan the next morning about the test results, he was disturbed. The normal range for the test was 1-5. The highest he had seen was a 10. Karan's results came back as a 13.9. Taking her hand, he said softly to her, "You are fortunate. The sudden onset of this disorder could have killed you."

Bipolar disorder is another name for manic-depression. Emotional fluctuations that affect individuals with bipolar disorder range from being manic, or high, to being extremely depressed. Upon questioning the physician further, Karan learned that she had carried the genetic disposition for bipolar disorder from birth, a recessive gene transmitted by her father. For twenty-eight years the gene remained inactive, but through stress, lack of sleep, normal depression and perhaps other contributing factors, the gene became activated.

She also learned that the sudden onset of bipolar disorder was rare. Normal onset occurred later in life, and over a period of weeks, even months. However, in Karan's case the event took place in a matter of seconds, perhaps prompted by contributing factors and caused by a massive and sudden infusion of blood into the brain under very high pressure.

Once Karan had found the cause of her memory loss and subsequent deep depression, the disorder could be treated. Psychiatrists put her on several medications, experimenting with each to find the correct drug and dosage to counteract the bipolar symptoms.

For the next three years Karan went through depression experimentation. Drug combinations took a toll on her body, her emotions and her mind. For every drug, there was a corresponding reaction. Doctors attempted to balance two chemicals in her body, serotonin and norepinephrine. Both chemicals allow for the normal processing of messages sent to the brain by the body. For victims of bipolar disorder, the brain discontinues the production of these two normal chemicals, leaving the victim in either a manic state or very depressed.

Karan's loss of memory took seven months to fully return. It was a traumatic time for her. As her memory returned, she would receive sharp, painful flashes that would cause her eyes to burn and hurt. The flashes brought back her past, piece by painful piece. Karan and Christine, her psychologist, recorded the images in a journal as they returned to Karan, slowly reconstructing a life that she had so suddenly lost.

She discovered that she had a genetic disposition for her illness, passed by a recessive gene from her father to her. She also learned that she would never recover from this disorder. It would be with her for the rest of her life. The medications put her on a roller-coaster of highs and lows, with often painful and serious side effects, but she would learn in the months that followed her onset with this disorder, that mental illness carries a much heavier burden with it than just an internal one.

As a nurse, and a professional caregiver, it was easier for Karan to accept the mental illness than for others. Her parents adamantly disapproved of Karan's seeing a psychologist for assistance. They even had a problem with Karan's being admitted to the psychiatric ward of the hospital following her memory loss. Karan knew what their reaction would be, and even asked the medical staff that her parents not be allowed to visit her while she was hospitalized. Her efforts were unsuccessful, however, as her father signed in as a minister and was therefore given access to her. With him was Karan's mother. When they walked into her room, Karan immediately recognized them.

"My mother immediately apologized for everything that she had ever done," Karan remembers painfully. "She internalized this disorder as being her fault. While I was the one who needed medical attention, it was I who was trying to help her cope. She definitely didn't help my situation at all."

Mental illness just wasn't something that Karan's parents were willing to accept, and insisted that she see a regular medical physician rather than a psychiatrist. It took Karan several days to get her parents to realize why she needed a psychiatrist. Using the example of her mother's knee surgery, Karan rationalized that her mother wouldn't have seen a regular family practitioner to perform the knee surgery. The example helped her parents adjust to the terrible sound of: psychiatrist.

Being diagnosed as suffering from bipolar disorder, Karan's professional career took a nosedive. The skilled nursing facility's owner wanted her fired. According to what Karan learned, the owners did not want a director of nursing with a "mental disease." They cited in her medical record that Karan had a nervous breakdown and therefore they had grounds to immediately fire her. They cleaned out her desk within days of her incident, but the administrator found a stack of time cards showing the overtime hours that Karan had actually worked during the past several months.

Although fired from her job, Karan was able to receive her overtime compensation – a compensation that paid her for almost the next seven months.

Those months were terribly difficult. Used to hard work and long hours, Karan now found herself unable to work and with too much free time on her hands. She realized quickly that her mental illness permeated every facet of her life. With no career, Karan lost her self-esteem and confidence. Her friends abandoned her; even her parents looked at her differently, as though Karan were fragile and breakable.

Karan often felt fragile herself. Every day brought new challenges, new fears. She spent her days at the library, reading every publication and book she could find on mental illness, depression and bipolar disease. Although understanding this disease gave her some solace, the depression seemed to engulf her and take on a life of its own. She often felt as if she were in a black hole, a void, where nothing but despair lived. All too frequently she felt suicidal, without hope.

Karan went weekly to therapy. She met others suffering from a variety of mental disorders. They became her only friends and her only support system. Each patient would share his or her experiences with the others, as did Karan. She fought to keep it together, but everything in her life had suddenly changed. From one moment of memory loss, she had become a totally different person. She had no job, no friends, was heavily medicated, struggling to understand, and at times, struggling for her own sanity.

Karan learned by experience that being mentally ill was viewed quite differently than being physically ill. She often felt as if the entire world was looking at her, seeing her disease, observing her being manic-depressive.

To put her life back together, Karan decided to move from Kentucky and near her brother, who lived in North Carolina. The move was good for her. She could put part of her life behind and perhaps start anew.

"I moved to North Carolina and went to the local hospital who was desperately looking for nurses. I told them in the interview that I didn't do overtime, wouldn't do primary care and would only stay three months." They hired her just the same; telling her that if she didn't like the work they would give her a plane ticket home after the three months had passed. They typed up the plane ticket and put it in her file, a recruitment tool that the hospital was using for recruiting nurses from out of state. The day before Christmas they presented Karan with the plane ticket and sent her home for two weeks. Karan ended up staying for eighteen years at this facility as a cardiac care nurse.

In addition to her duties as a floor nurse, Karan took a special interest in patients suffering from depression and bipolar disease. She befriended everyone that she could, and volunteered her time at therapy sessions, in patients' homes, and speaking on the telephone with individuals at night and on weekends.

"Talking someone through the process is very important," Karan says of newly diagnosed patients. "It is important for people to know they are not going crazy and can put their lives back together, as I had done."

Karan met her husband in 1995. He was a fellow employee at the hospital who was in an unhappy marriage. When he finally became divorced, Karan sent him a card that said "I've been admiring you from afar for a long time. If you would like to go out on a blind date, please ask the floor nurse for my telephone number. The poor man had no idea who had sent the card to him, but retrieved her telephone number and went out on the blind date. Two-and-a-half years later Walter and Karan were married.

At first, the marriage was everything that Karan had dreamed of: a life companion, support for her own depression and disease and financial help with two incomes. The couple decided not to have children. They knew that the gene for bipolar disorder would be passed on.

In 1999, Walter was diagnosed with bipolar disease as well. His disease manifested slower, but he began to suffer from age regression, becoming like an infant again. Medication could help him deal with the depression cycles, but the regression was more difficult to treat. In time, Karan had to leave her nursing position to care for her husband.

"He would sit on the floor and rock back and forth saying, 'cold, cold, cold.' I would have to wrap him in a blanket and rock him, just as though he were an infant." His bipolar manifestation required almost constant supervision. While Walter went in and out of age regression stages, Karan had no idea when episodes would begin, or what the triggers were. She had little choice but to stay with him all day, every day.

Karan relates that her husband's age regression went through infancy, two, three, four, five, six and seven years old. She manages a weak smile as she recalls that her husband got stuck as an eight-year-old, relating how he would line up his GI-Joe soldiers and play army for hours at a time. Karan relates that as she came and went through the day, she wasn't allowed to touch any of the army trucks or soldiers, because Walter knew where every truck and soldier had been placed.

For years, Karan had managed her own depression through awareness, medication and internal fortitude, but this was even more frustrating because she had little control over his disease. She took her husband to her psychiatrist and treatment for Walter's bipolar disorder began. The cost of such treatment, now for both, was staggering.

"Walter would go through the terrible twos, and have angry temper tantrums, throwing things across the floor. Never at me, but still disruptive." Friends and even hospital staff members were concerned for Karan's safety, even suggesting that she divorce him. She has stayed with him, however, fighting her own depression and now, fighting his as well.

It was yet another challenge in Karan's already challenging existence. With no income from her husband or herself, the couple fell on hard economic times.

With nowhere else to turn, Karan takes her husband to the County Mental Health Clinic every day. He is on total disability, but the income covers only a few of the bills. Walter is progressing well as therapy continues and according to Karan, he has reached a state in his mid-twenties, a far cry from his beginning age regression.

The future is bleak for Karan and Walter. Medications for the couple cost over $1600 a month. Neither Karan nor Walter can work. They have no insurance. Without some assistance, they would simply be unable to survive economically. Karan's savings were depleted quickly after her husband became ill and they were forced to apply for Medicaid coverage for him. With the help of Karan's psychiatrist, Karan was qualified to be put on an indigent program to help pay medical bills that would cripple any American family.

Because of bipolar disease the couple must live in need of assistance. There is no other way to survive. Even with medicines and medical assistance paid for, the couple faces almost certain bankruptcy. Bill collectors harass them, the paperwork for medical assistance almost buries them and then, there is their disease to cope with every moment of their lives. Karan has applied for disability assistance, but the wait is long. She has been turned down twice for benefits and has been forced to pay an attorney for help.

"We do the best we can," Karan offers. "It simply isn't easy to cope, but we've managed. Somehow we've managed."

Karan's Story
Coping with Bipolar Disorder

Expect to Grieve

The National Institute of Mental Health estimates that 8% of the U.S. population suffers from bipolar disorder, but as Karan states, "You feel like you are the only person alive with this disease."

For Karan and her husband, the onset of bipolar disorder was life changing. No aspect of her life was unaffected. Successfully dealing with mental illness of any kind often means, "beginning a new life," Karan says. With her old life gone, grief was inevitable. "I quickly realized that I wasn't even the same person that I was before. I was devastated and grieved long and hard.

She offers the same advice to anyone with an onset of mental illness: "Allow yourself to grieve." Karan immediately sought ongoing professional therapy to resolve her questions, get needed medications and to deal with her grief and anger.

A Life of Restrictions

While bipolar disorder is treatable, it can also leave a life in total disruption. Therapists and physicians all set new restrictions on Karan's life. For her, the effects were so dramatic that she wouldn't return to work for months. She was simply unable to. These restrictions forced her to set new goals that would seem small and insignificant to others.

While medication was helpful to curb the highs and lows of mania and depression, Karan learned to recognize new boundaries in her life. To gain control of her life again, Karan needed to know how high the highs would be and how low the lows would take her.

"I found myself demonstrating very odd behavior at times," Karan says. "I would go from a very elevated, promising mood to being despondent and grumpy within minutes. "It seemed that nothing in particular would trigger these mood swings, but she likened the adjustment as learning to walk again. "Just when I thought I might take a step forward and do something proactive in my life, I would fall back in self-doubt and paranoia before I could reach the door."

Triggers for Karan were things to be avoided: stress, worry, anxiety, and loud discussions with friends or relationships, among others. Because bipolar disorder often accentuates erratic mood swings of behavior, Karan had a difficult time distinguishing what was real and what was imagined. "Early on, I really thought I was losing my mind completely."

Focusing on the smallest of projects was difficult for her. Financial concerns and emotional instability added to her growing dilemma. Goals and dreams in her former life were simply unattainable now.

"You learn early on that you need to replan your life, set small goals, like taking shortened steps before longer strides."

The adjustment was difficult. She felt alone and isolated. "Only the closest of friends and family members stayed with me," Karan recalls. "That was probably the hardest adjustment for me to make. I was still Karan, but somehow, no one else thought so!"

Use Caution in Making Decisions

For Karan, advice poured in from every source, including highly unlikely ones. It seemed everyone knew what was best for her, even if they had no clue as to what they were speaking of. That is where Karan started studying at the public library. "I read everything about bipolar that I could. I just had to believe that I could get quick and adequate treatment."

"Beware of the 'know-it-alls' who seem to know what is best for you!" Advice ranged from sleeping more hours in the day to working hard and getting adequate rest. Medications caused side effects that she had not expected. She was forced to learn to cope with these side effects, just as she had to cope with the disease itself. Her self-esteem was deeply affected, because of this she knew that she must develop more dependency to others than she was comfortable with.

"Emotionally I was so hurt. I sat and cried for hours on end. Other times I would be content to sit and do nothing. I was often suicidal. It was awful."

Dealing with her condition was bad enough, but Karan was now faced with a formidable foe in the "system" in which she now found herself. The medical system was a maze that she still hasn't gotten accustomed to negotiating. Insurance companies and medical offices seemed to be working at opposite ends, all looking to Karan for answers she simply didn't have, and didn't even understand! "Medical clerks treated me like some sort of moron. It infuriated me. The adage of 'hurry up and wait,' certainly applies to medicine, and even more appropriate to insurance companies!"

"Use caution when making decisions about your future," Karan says softly. "Not everyone is looking out for your best interests."

Family Abuse
The Deep Scars of Incest...

...Cynthia's Story

Abuse within the family is considered one of the most crippling causes of invisible disabilities to a child. While there are few statistics that accurately portray the scope of the severe abuse of children within the family, no one doubts the negative impact it has on a human life.

Emotional, physical, sexual and psychological abuse of children by parents, guardians, siblings and extended family members can have a lifelong effect on a child and can result in debilitating invisible scars and disabilities.

Child sexual abuse is any form of sexual activity with a child when there is no consent or when consent is not possible. Perpetrators are most often someone whom the child knows and quite often trusts. The perpetrator often has easy access to the child. Abuse of any nature occurs in every race, religion, culture and country.

The effects of child sexual abuse vary widely depending on the severity of the abuse, the age of the child, length and frequency of perpetuation and the nature of the relationship. In most cases, the emotional effects include: confusion, powerlessness, pain, betrayal, depression, anger, panic, anxiety, sadness, feeling unsafe, suspicion of others, grief, a deep sense of loss and feeling miserable. If the abuse happens very early in life the child may have no conscious memory of the abuse, but still feel the deep effects. For most children, they are forever changed and affected by sexual abuse.

Tragically, most abused children feel unloved and unlovable. They can feel dirty, ashamed, unworthy or that they are bad. Survivors are often confronted with overwhelming pain as they try to cope with the intense emotions and grief from abuse. Many victims will minimize these internal emotions or rationalize them away. Still others will deny the memory or block the abuse from their conscious minds. Others may dissociate, or feel that they were not really there during the abusive episodes.

Because a person's boundaries were not respected, they were utterly violated. It may be difficult to find and maintain new boundaries as the child grows up, leaving the survivor continually vulnerable to further abuse. Survivors often grow up trusting no one, or have difficulty in normal human relations because of the abuse on them.

Sexual abuse of the child's body can lead to severe challenges with their bodies as the child grows to adulthood. Attempting to cope with pain, the survivor may develop eating disorders, have an inability to enjoy sex, have self-destructive behaviors, display promiscuous behavior or develop gender-identity issues. The effects of sexual abuse go so deep that a child may go to any lengths to avoid the pain, possibly resulting in depression and suicide. Addictions are common; isolation, compulsive behaviors, and anger management might become major issues as an adult, making day-to-day life activity very difficult. To respond to abuse, these behaviors are learned and serve a very important function – survival.

Survivors of sexual or severe physical abuse have difficult adjustments to make as they reach adulthood. Some make them because they seek help. Others endure life with their pain in the best fashion they can. Still others, sadly, do not deal with their pain well and can inflict much pain on others and themselves for the remainder of their lives. Many survivors, however, grow to be highly sensitive, loving and compassionate adults.

One such individual is Cynthia.

Cynthia's Story
Family Abuse...

...The Deep Scars of Incest

It is often the worst type of disability, least understood and often carries the strongest public bias – the invisible disability. The chronic emotional, physical or mental pain, that no one can see, touch, feel or heal. For millions of Americans, invisible disabilities force them out of work, into retirement, or in the case of some, they might not receive the opportunity to work at all.

Cynthia's story illustrates the frustration, public mistrust and misunderstanding with an unseen disability.

She grew up with seven siblings in rural North Carolina. Her father was a carpenter and her mother took care of the children in the home. Although Cynthia didn't know it then, she grew up in rural poverty. During lean times, she remembers her mother making fried biscuits with Karo syrup and coffee. Everyone at the table ate, but all too often there was little else that the family had to eat. Biscuits were made from flour and water and dropped into a pan of hot grease.

Cynthia remembers being observant of how her father took care of the household and helped supplement the family by having a garden. She was equally observant of her mother. Cynthia helped her cook, and take care of the younger ones, among many other household tasks. She was a fast learner. There was a family secret however, a hurtful and devastating family secret. A member of her family had sexually abused her. The molestation had taken place just as Cynthia began to develop, roughly twelve or thirteen and had continued on and off for over a year. She had blocked much of it from her memory, even as a young teen, but haunting images remained. When she confronted her mother, she received the reply, "You should have been a boy."

Even a neighbor, married with children, had tried to molest her. Cynthia didn't share these experiences with anyone. She felt shame, somehow responsible, dirty and unworthy. These negative emotions were perpetuated through much of her life, leaving Cynthia with a profound lack of self worth.

From an early age, Cynthia was overweight from a limited diet of mostly fats and carbohydrates. It seemed she couldn't escape the jokes and teasing played on her at school. She was called derogatory names, and laughed at by the other children. Because of Cynthia's larger sizes, her mother often made her clothes. To earn money for fabric, Cynthia was made to work at an early age. She did odd jobs in town or for other residents of the tiny North Carolina town in which she was raised.

"I remember all the names as though it were yesterday," Cynthia says with sadness. "I was called Fatso, El-Porko, Chunky Meat, Hippopotamus, Elephant Girl, Bertha Butt, you name it." In school, Cynthia sat by herself because none of the other students wanted to be around her. To soothe her wounds and hurt, Cynthia ate. She found a few other students like her, "rejects," she called them and they became her friends, children she could play with or trust in.

From her first memories, Cynthia could recall being laughed at. The jokes, name calling and teasing always hurt, tearing at her self-esteem and her heart. It started in elementary school and got progressively worse in middle school and high school. Dances hurt the worst. The rejection from other students made her feel terrible.

"While in high school I began to be aware of why these kids teased me and poked fun of me so," Cynthia says with insight. "They were just as scared and insecure as I was, but I was the easiest to pick on and it made them feel bigger and more self-worthy. It gave them some purpose."

Life at home didn't offer Cynthia much relief. Being the heaviest of eight children brought the same cruelty down on Cynthia at home as she felt in school. The constant teasing and barrage of hurtful comments to her would often cause Cynthia to fight back, which would rile her mother. This behavior led to severe spankings for Cynthia. She received more than her share from her father as well. Cynthia's remembers him as a man with a short and violent temper. If he saw two of his children fighting both received beatings.

"We were a poor family. People teased me because I was poor and couldn't afford store-bought clothes," Cynthia says. "A lot of our clothes were secondhand and we did what we could to get by. My mother could sew very well and taught me as well. Later in her life, it turned into a good business for her."

Although her family was poor, Cynthia knew that her parents did the best they could. "We loved our father. When he would come home from work on Friday after getting paid, he'd often bring us a piece of candy, something to make us feel good, and that we were special." However her father was quick to show anger. If he saw something not being done his way, Cynthia recalls, he would often go off the "deep end," growing violently angry. She knows that he had unduly difficult financial pressure on him, but she will never forget that when he got angry with her, he always called her, "stupid."

"It was like a constant with him. When he was angry, we (Cynthia, brothers and sisters) were constantly called stupid. He was my daddy, why would I doubt him? I guess I was not stupid, but inside of me I was always trying to please him."

Cynthia had no close friends. No one would eat with her at school, so she sat alone. There were a few kids whom she could talk to, but most were outcasts like her. She gravitated to adults, who were often more accepting than the kids that she was around in school. "I had several friends who were bus drivers," she recalls. "I looked up to them and they wouldn't laugh at me. They were kind of free spirited I guess and didn't seem to get into the teasing much."

To cope with the constant name-calling, Cynthia escaped with drugs and alcohol in high school. She began to drink heavily, binge drinking whenever the opportunity arose. She also started smoking marijuana. Occasionally at first, but as her unhappiness grew, so did her habit. By the time she was a junior in high school, she was selling drugs to others. Her drinking and smoking often were done with the bus drivers. While she had interest in boys during high school, she didn't date. At her senior prom, Cynthia remembers sitting the entire time alone until near the end of the night a boy who had come alone asked her for a dance. For a brief moment she felt pretty, but after the dance, she was alone again.

Although she was troubled, Cynthia was the first of her siblings to finish high school. In time, only two of the eight children would even graduate from high school. She remembers getting little help at home with any high school project, and rarely had a quiet atmosphere to study in. "There was very little privacy."

"The smoking and drinking helped calm me down," Cynthia recalls. "I was so hurt most of the time, angry some of the time and alone, most of the time." Just after graduation Cynthia was kicked out of the house. The considerable strain between her and her parents had worsened. She was tired of the verbal and physical abuse and when her mother told her to leave, Cynthia did. She moved in with her older sister in Charlotte and her drinking and drug use escalated. Her sister had gotten married to get out of the house, and her home was the only place for Cynthia to go.

"Eating was a gratification issue with me. As my sense of unworthiness grew, so did my body size. I rewarded myself for the smallest things during my day with eating. I can remember that if I talked to my mother or father and they said something good about me, my eyes would water and I would almost start crying. But I didn't have a very good relationship with my mother and father after I left home. If I felt depressed because of a hurtful comment, I ate. If I had a bad day and was feeling particularly bad about something I had done, I ate. It was a vicious and never-ending cycle of self-abuse."

To make ends meet, Cynthia worked twelve-to-fourteen-hour days at her job. While the teasing about her weight had slowed since her days in high school, she nevertheless felt society's bias against overweight people. Drinking and drug use continued for Cynthia after high school and after she had left home. Even her eating disorder worsened, leading to binging often for reward or for anger. Cynthia didn't realize that her pain was justifying her overeating. Cynthia left home when she was seventeen.

"I knew I could succeed at something. I started an assistant manger training program at Pizza Hut and had been in the program for six of the nine weeks when the manager I worked for was fired and a new manager was hired. He never liked me. He made my life hell. He tried to get rid of me; he wanted me to quit. Finally it came to a head and I came to work one morning to find the locks had been changed on the door. I was out of a job. Cynthia feels racial bias made these events occur and wondered if the "wheel of rejection" would ever end?"

Cynthia had now felt the pain of obesity prejudice her entire life. From school days, relationships and now at work, she was treated as a second-class citizen, someone lower and more unworthy of work or promotion than another person.

During her year at Pizza Hut Cynthia moved in with a young man whom she thought was the "love of my life." They were not alone in the house they moved to, however, and it turned out to be a drug house. "The drinking and drugs relaxed me and chilled me out." Cynthia was in love, and being loved in return. For the first time in her life she felt special and accepted, but when the relationship ended because of the drug situation in the house, Cynthia moved back home. She was pregnant.

It was then that Cynthia had to deal with another serious incident in her life. Two weeks after she moved, Cynthia had a miscarriage and lost her baby. She cried for six months over the loss of the baby and her boyfriend. Every night she cried herself to sleep. "I think it was the drugs that helped cause the miscarriage. I had stopped using everything as soon as I learned I was pregnant, but I believe to this day that I lost the child because of the drugs."

Cynthia's advice to other victims of incest, offered years later, is to realize that it wasn't your fault, get the help you need, and don't retreat into yourself or start using drugs or alcohol to soothe the pain. "I put myself on a plateau where I didn't have to deal with it," she says. "If you don't get help, professional help, you may find yourself pulling back, not sleeping, trying to cope on your own, perhaps moving from job to job, or relationship to relationship."

Cynthia blames the incest on her inability to have stable and healthy relationships with men. "I wonder now if that is the reason why I couldn't stop eating as well. Perhaps eating was a self-preservation mechanism to push people away and therefore find me unattractive."

After a short time, Cynthia moved from her parents' house and into her own place. She found work in factories near or in Charlotte. "I always did my work well and got promoted quickly. I was a fast learner but I had an ongoing problem with some male supervisors. At times I felt sexually harassed because I wouldn't put up with them. I remember one job I interviewed for, the man said he wouldn't hire me because I was overweight. I look back now, and wish I had known my rights and stood up for myself instead of being abused in the workplace also."

Cynthia managed to not lose her place in all of this. She rarely got discouraged, and always felt that every incident, positive or negative had a purpose. "I always felt I was pushed forward. Even though one part of any situation is detrimental, the other helps you cope." Cynthia credits her Christian faith in helping get her through the tough times.

Through the years, Cynthia has grown to be accepting of others, even those that have hurt her.

She has learned that accepting others shouldn't depend on one's body size, or type of job, beauty, or any of the normal things people consider. She believes that a person must look beyond the "cover" into the "book" itself. While severely damaged by the incestuous episodes in her life, she holds no grudges or animosity. "Doing so," she says, "would only add to the pain, not to the solution."

Invisible disabilities run deep. They are the cause of physical, emotional and psychological trauma. For Cynthia, the pain started young and just continued. Although she has worked throughout most of her life, Cynthia never received the job training she needed to get the career she wanted or deserved. She felt that she didn't have the education or direction she needed to succeed. Eventually she filed for disability benefits. When she was referred to Goodwill Industries by Vocational Rehabilitation, she came without much knowledge of computers and had poor typing skills. It was an appropriate course of study for her and soon she was enrolled in Goodwill's computer skills series, classes that took her from the basics to more complicated programs which taught her word processing, spread sheets, resume preparation and typing skills, among many other subjects covered in this series.

"I guess I just needed encouragement," Cynthia says of the training staff at Goodwill. "They have not only taught me computer skills, but have reinforced the belief that I am worthy, and I am a good person."

Although Cynthia received disability income, she needed the assistance until she could land the job she wanted. She pioneered the medical transcription program at Goodwill, and was the first graduate of the program.

"Cynthia always was ready for the next challenge," says Meg Green, who assisted Cynthia in computer training at Goodwill. "She was eager, hungry in fact to learn. An ideal student."

Individuals with less resolve than Cynthia would simply have given up. She has considered it herself, but ultimately, Cynthia was the first to be at the classes at Goodwill and the last to leave. She knew she needed a better job but with back pain and other physical problems, her days of restaurant employment, plant work and management were realistically over.

"I can't thank the staff at Goodwill enough," she says. "They don't force feed this training, they assume you will do it on your own. I don't know about everyone else, but it's the chance I needed. I can do it on my own. I believe in the saying that 'the only time you fail is when you quit trying.' So my advice to everyone is not to give up. Keep pushing to the top, you can break the limitations of your disability. There is a world out there with others like you that have made it. Always believe in that."

Family Abandonment
A Painful Trend...

...Bernadette's Story

When a couple falls in love and marries, most consider it to be forever. Mutual love turns their romance into a family and young ones look to both mother and father for guidance, love and support. Children need the influence of both parents to be well adjusted, but often, too often, those children will be left with a single parent with whom to be raised.

The single-parent family is not new on society's landscape. The last three decades have all but redefined what the family even looks like. Well over half of the persons reading this will have come from a single-parent family, or have been raised in a step-parented family. Stepfamilies have become commonplace and well accepted in our society, but what of the children who are left, abandoned by a father or mother? What scars are left upon those spouses and children?

This is Bernadette's story.

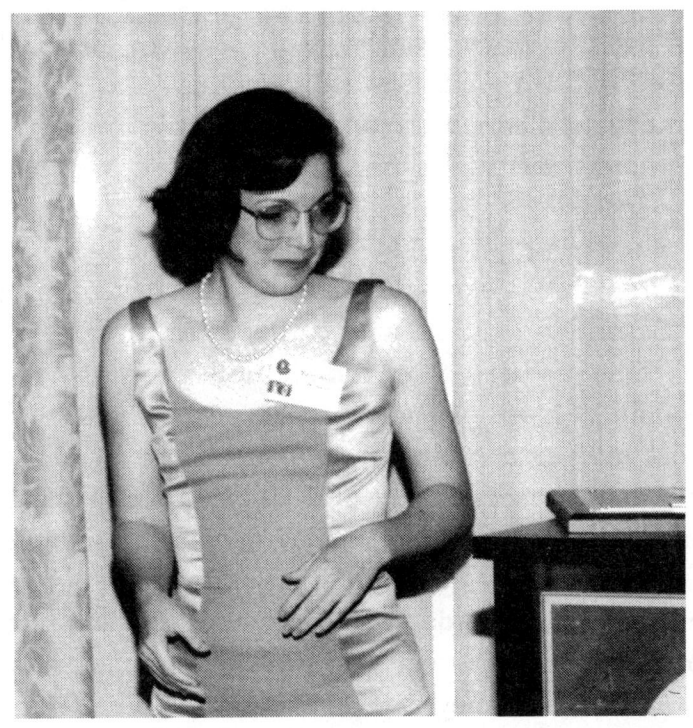

Bernadette's Story
Family Abandonment...

...A Painful Trend

Bernadette was living the fantasy life of many young women: three adorable and intelligent children, a hard-working husband who loved her, and a stay-at-home job being a mom. During the day she took her kids on walks, took them to the park, and to the town library. She read to them. She played with them. Toward evening, she prepared dinner and cleaned the apartment while awaiting her husband's arrival from work. Life was good for Bernadette.

But gradually, life began to change. Three children and a house to maintain is a full-time job, so Bernadette didn't notice the signs her husband was giving her. She didn't notice that he was becoming more withdrawn. She shrugged off his short temper and darker moods, telling herself that he was stressed from work. Even when he started coming home later and later from work, she believed his stories that the job was becoming more demanding. Bernadette had her children, her house, and her small, "perfect" world.

Although money was tight for the young married couple, it would have been difficult for Bernadette to work outside of the house. Daycare for three children cost almost as much as Bernadette could make with her limited skills. So the couple struggled from week to week providing as best as they could. There was little money left over for recreation.

The couple's credit cards added to their financial misery. Kids' clothes and other incidentals were simply not covered with one paycheck. They used credit cards to take a family vacation, to purchase glasses and buy clothes and shoes. Soon the high interest cards were at their maximum expenditures.

The couple could only afford minimum payments and the cycle of debt grew deeper and deeper.

One particular Friday, Bernadette watched as her husband got out of his truck and walked through the front door. He looked tired and said to her that they needed to talk. She sat beside him and he explained that the company had asked him to accept a transfer from Florida to North Carolina. He told her that the company would help with some moving expenses, but he wanted her to take the kids and go by train to begin house hunting. Supportive as always, Bernadette agreed and reassured him that she and the kids would manage. She was even excited that he had decided to move to Greensboro, where her mother lived. Her husband informed her that he would work out the remainder of next week, then join her in North Carolina the following weekend, if she could find a place to live in the meantime. Bernadette's mother lived in a one-bedroom apartment and therefore could not accommodate her grandchildren and daughter.

Over the weekend he shared with Bernadette that he wanted her and the kids to take the train to North Carolina and begin to look for a place to live. He told her that he would make hotel reservations for her and the kids, buy her the train tickets and give her money. Bernadette agreed and the kids were excited about the upcoming adventure, also about spending time with their grandmother.

They left Florida early in the week. With a hug from her husband, Bernadette took her children and boarded the train for North Carolina. She had only $15 cash in her pocket and his promise of a hotel room reserved for them in Greensboro. With trepidation, and a strange sense of fear in her heart, she looked back to see her husband walking away from the train station.

The children walked through all of the cars, and were mesmerized by the sound of the wheels clacking through the night. They slept in their seats. As they rested, Bernadette's heart grew heavier as the miles took her farther and farther away from her Florida home. She felt something was not right, but finally closed her eyes and fell into a restless sleep.

As they left the train early the next morning Bernadette placed a call to Florida from the train station. Her husband wasn't home. She simply wanted to tell him that they had arrived. She called his work number, but was told he had not been there. Her worry intensified. Where could he have gone? Putting a smile back on her face she turned to her kids, took their hands and walked confidently out of the station. Her mother waited for them outside the depot.

Bernadette set about her journey through town, gathering papers and apartment guides, as she had been asked to do. The children were having a wonderful time. Everything was new to them. Bernadette made the event an adventure for the kids.

However in her heart, she was feeling more troubled. Why wasn't he at work? If he were not there, why wouldn't he be at home? She called again, and then again. Before the day was out, she had tried repeatedly to find him, but got the same answer from his company – he wasn't at work.

By the end of the first day, Bernadette's deepest fears were being realized. There was no hotel reservation as he had promised, nor were there funds in the bank to use the ATM machine. She was denied use of the credit cards she carried; all were at or over the limit. She had left messages both at their home and at his workplace. There were no messages on her mother's phone. She heard only an ominous silence from Florida and her heart became paralyzed with fear.

She borrowed some money from her father and moved herself and the kids into an extended stay hotel near the interstate. There she tried to sort out the truth. She sat in the middle of the night, all three kids together sleeping in the bed, and pondered her fate. Was she so unlovable? Why had he deserted her? Perhaps he was missing, hurt or even dead. Every possible scenario ran through her mind. She resisted the urge to borrow money for a plane ticket and fly home, to Florida. There must be a problem with him, she reasoned, but as she sat alone in the dark nights that followed, she remembered the many signals he had been sending her. She didn't want to believe it, but in the end she came to the only realization she could – he had simply left her.

The days were filled with trying to be brave for her children. Her nights, however, were another matter. Images of him came to her like thieves in the night, taking more of her self-esteem each time. She felt betrayed. She felt anger. She felt guilt. Mostly, she just felt fear. What was to become of them? How was she to care for herself and her children? Where would she live? Who would hire her?

Bernadette's situation was desperate. She had no money of her own, and the funds she had borrowed from her father were rapidly being spent. She knew that neither her father nor her mother had the money to help her for long. Her job skills were limited to a few temporary positions, and having no permanent address or even a phone to call her own, it would be difficult to find a suitable position enabling her to pay expenses. Most of all, she felt terribly alone and unloved. Relations with her mother had been strained over the years, and she knew that she couldn't rely on her mother for help much longer.

More than anything, Bernadette worried for her children. She couldn't rely on her mother to care for them because her mother worked. Daycare was simply out of the question. It was too expensive for three children. She worried to the point of lack of sleep, and finally realized that she simply had to start doing something – anything.

She made a list of things to do and started
checking them off. She knew that in order to survive,
however, she would need assistance. It wouldn't be
easy for her, but it was necessary. She would simply
have to swallow her pride and find assistance.

Bernadette started making calls from the hotel
room. She called every agency that might possibly
assist in helping her. She made progress when
someone suggested that she should call the
Greensboro Interfaith Hospitality Network. It was
after that call that Bernadette finally saw some light
at the end of her long, dark tunnel. The network was
part of a national organization dedicated to helping
homeless families to find a place to live. In
Greensboro, thirteen host churches took turns
letting three to five homeless families sleep in their
churches' classrooms and fellowship halls. The
churches provided the place to stay, prepared meals
and provided volunteers to aid the homeless families.
It was a blessing to Bernadette and her children.

"The program is incredible," Bernadette says.
"The women in there destroyed any of the stereotypes
I ever had about homelessness. They were all
employed, all self-confident. Just the smallest things
– they picked the wrong husbands, picked the wrong
roommate – put them in that position."

Finally secure in the knowledge that she had a
place to live and food to eat, Bernadette set her next
goal, that of finding a job. With the help of the
volunteers who ran the daycare center for free,

Bernadette had the flexibility of finally being free of the children for a few hours every day to hunt for a job. The Interfaith Hospitality Network sent Bernadette to the county's social services department who, in turn, referred Bernadette to Goodwill Industries. The Employment Works program at Goodwill offered Bernadette and others who needed a job a crash course in resume preparation, interviewing skills, building self-esteem and dressing for a successful interview. The five-day program was all that Bernadette really needed to get started. Job counselors and employment specialists within Goodwill then helped every enrollee in the Employment Works program to search for a suitable position. All that Goodwill asked of its participants was the desire to work at getting a job. There were no fees for any of the services Bernadette was offered while at Goodwill.

Slowly, Bernadette observed positive changes within herself. She was growing from a deferential housewife and stay-at-home mother to an assertive head of the household.

"I had to learn that there was nothing wrong or arrogant about being self-confident. From the way I dressed, or shook hands with someone, they coached me on all of this, telling me that it was necessary to finding a good job."

When Bernadette finished the Goodwill program she had been coached on interviewing skills, had a professionally prepared resume in hand, some new clothes and a large dose of self-confidence. With a smile on her face she began walking door-to-door in search of a job. Computer databases at Goodwill enabled her to follow up on positions listed on the Internet or specific employer websites. Job postings researched by Goodwill employment counselors also gave her leads. She walked and talked, left resumes and interviewed at every opportunity, regardless of the position.

It was hard work, perhaps harder than she had previously expected. After four weeks of diligence, however, her efforts paid off. She found clerical work in an attorney's office in the downtown area, not far from the church where she and her children lived.

"I think she's an amazing story of perseverance," said Clinton Thomas, vice president of Career Development Services at Goodwill Industries. "Here's someone who could have given up, could have remained on public assistance, but that's not what she wanted."

Working part-time hours at the attorney's office allowed Bernadette the time to enroll in the University of North Carolina – Greensboro. Because of the events that occurred in her life she decided to pursue a degree in human development and family studies. Within a short time, she and her children moved into a two-bedroom apartment near the campus.

For Bernadette, the courage she mustered to change her life came from the three children that loved her. "My kids are my everything. They are the reason I get up in the morning," Bernadette said. "There are two things I could choose to hold on to – my pride or my kids. I'm not embarrassed to ask for anything for them."

Her apartment is not fancy. All of the furniture is used, mainly from Goodwill. She has no car and must either walk to work and school or use public transportation. She needed food stamps for a while, and child-care vouchers, but didn't hesitate to take the help when she needed it. She did what she had to do to survive, one day at a time.

Life is more than mere survival for Bernadette now. She is filled with gratitude toward the many people who befriended her, assisted her and believed in her. She knows that it was not just a few people, but hundreds of people who didn't hesitate to offer assistance and help her toward self-sufficiency.

In a contemplative mood while home alone in her apartment, Bernadette looks up to the wall and sees the plaque that bears her name. She was honored by Goodwill at their annual meeting and presented with the Michael W. Haley Employment Works Graduate of the Year award. That award is a constant reminder to her of how far she has come since the day at the train depot with just $15 in her pocket.

"I have always been a work-hard, pull-yourself-up-by-the-bootstraps type of person," Bernadette says of her journey, "But it's nice to have the boots first."

Cerebral Palsy
A Crippling Disability...

...Debbie's Story

Cerebral palsy was first diagnosed in the mid-1800s by English surgeon William Little. The condition was called Little's Disease for many years and described the crippling disease that affected children in their first years of life causing stiff, spastic muscles in their legs and, to a lesser degree, their arms. These children had difficulty grasping objects, crawling and walking. For many years, the cause of cerebral palsy was considered to be a lack of oxygen to the brain of the fetus during birth. The blockage or shortage of oxygen damaged brain tissue, causing loss of mobility and spastic diplegia.

During research in the 1980s it was discovered that oxygen blockage at birth caused a relatively small number of cases of cerebral palsy at birth. The actual cause for almost 90% of the cases, two to four births per 1,000 in the United States, is still unknown. What is known is that some conditions such as jaundice and rubella (German measles) can cause cerebral palsy, conditions that are easily treatable before the child is affected. But much more work is needed as to the cause.

The term cerebral refers to the brain's two halves and palsy describes any disorder that impairs control of bodily movement. Thus, these disorders are not caused by problems in the muscles or nerves. Damage to motor areas in the brain that disrupt the brain's ability to adequately control movement and posture causes this disorder.

Cerebral palsy is not contagious nor is it usually inherited. At the present time there is no known cure for the condition, although scientific research continues to yield improved treatments and methods of prevention.

The United Cerebral Palsy Association estimates more than 500,000 Americans have cerebral palsy. While research has improved treatment, the number of births every year that result in cerebral palsy continues to be about the same as it was thirty years ago. Infants born with the condition often have multiple disorders such as mental impairment (about one third of cases), seizures or epilepsy (as many as half of births).

Normal growth patterns are often lacking in children with cerebral palsy, making this disorder especially difficult for parents. Children often take longer to crawl, walk or speak and usually have abnormal sensation and perception problems as well as impaired vision or hearing.

For more information about cerebral palsy, readers may access:

- National Institute of Health (NINDS), www.ninds.nih.gov
- United Cerebral Palsy Association, www.ucpa.org
- March of Dimes Birth Defects Foundation, www.modimes.org
- National Easter Seal Society, www.easter-seals.org

Debbie's Story
Cerebral Palsy...

...A Crippling Disability

Debbie makes her way tentatively across the work floor at Goodwill Industries. She has difficulty walking and has fallen from time to time. It is equally as hard to control her arms and hands as she packages products and handles cardboard.

Speaking is difficult for her and she often labors to be understood by others.

Debbie has cerebral palsy. She has had it since birth.

In addition to unbalanced walking, it is hard for Debbie to write. Uncontrollable twitching of her arms makes coordinated hand movements difficult. Given her range of disabilities, most work would simply be out of the question for her. However, her mind functions with ease. She has wit and a wonderful sense of humor. As many of us do, Debbie longs to find that special someone and get married.

She has three siblings, two sisters and a brother, none of whom suffer from cerebral palsy as does Debbie. All have stayed close to Debbie over the years, especially her brother. But without her mother's daily devotion to her daughter, Debbie would probably have been institutionalized years earlier. Mother and daughter spend much together, eating out, shopping and going back and forth to work at Goodwill. They are best friends. For Debbie, her mother is a lifeline to a normal life.

At her birth, there were complications. Debbie was born with an opening in the windpipe that had to be surgically repaired. She was three months in the hospital.

While many children born with cerebral palsy do not walk, Debbie began walking at three and enrolled in a special school for disabled children during the same year. The Gateway Education School specialized in many disabilities, but paramount to their education curriculum was teaching children with cerebral palsy. By age fourteen, pressure to mainstream children with disabilities was strong and Debbie entered middle school. It was not a good time for her.

"I was teased and laughed at," Debbie recalls her first weeks in a public middle school. "It hurt me so much."

Debbie's erratic twitching, unsteady gait and difficult speech stood out among the teenagers who were often preoccupied with looks and physical prowess. Although she had the ability to learn as fast and as well as her middle school students, Debbie was constantly hurt by their quick laughs, furtive stares and derogatory comments.

Her stay in middle school was short. The few months were hard on her and she recalls the hurt with vivid memory. From public school, Debbie was enrolled into the technical college and took adult classes, often with others that had disabilities.

When Debbie was seventeen she was referred to the county sheltered workshop. The sheltered workshop provided work experience from which Debbie could earn a paycheck and some self-respect. She remained employed at the workshop, now known as Lifespan for eighteen years. Her daily life consisted of light packaging and repetitive tasks that Debbie could perform. She worked with individuals with a variety of disabilities and made friends, all of which she was very proud of.

Following her working years at Lifespan, Debbie came to Goodwill as a part time employee working in the Commercial Services department which does work for community businesses. Debbie likes her job at Goodwill for a variety of reasons, and says most of the Goodwill consumers who work alongside of her are high functioning individuals with physical disabilities.

Debbie's strength doesn't come from her body. It isn't even her keen intellect. Her strength comes from within her, a quiet resolve to work hard, share life with others and be grateful for all the blessings she does possess. Debbie is quick to add that most important on the list is her faith and her church.

At home she is active with computer games, on line bingo (not for money), and occasionally chatting on the Internet with her friends. She listens to her favorite oldies on the radio and spends time with her mother.

Like most of us, Debbie wishes to meet a person who will accept her and perhaps some day she can even marry. That effort has made Debbie an advocate for an on-line dating service for persons with disabilities. The service operates from Tuscon, Arizona and is called, Differently Abled Winner's Network (D.A.W.N.) The service operates for about five hundred members nationwide and reaches out specifically, but not exclusively, for the "differently abled" population.

Through the service, Debbie has been matched with several individuals. Members list their likes, dislikes, special needs, goals and expectations and are then matched with similar individuals. For Debbie, it has brought special friendships and acceptance, including several boyfriends. It also brought her to Randy, a special friend who also suffers from cerebral palsy. She has known Randy for five years and talks frequently with him by telephone and email. While they have never met in person, Debbie hopes that one day they might. She has never lost hope for a married life, even with her crippling disability.

As for her employment at Goodwill, Debbie has found a home. "People treat me good here and the pay is good as well. This is a very good place to work."

Debbie has lived a challenging life. A life that few could understand. Trapped in a body that does not function as well as most, Debbie's obstacles have been profound. Even the most common of functions, such as eating or drinking is hard for her. Yet, she has never given up on her dreams or her desire to live as normal a life as she can. Her presence reminds all of those who know her just how much we all take for granted.

No story of Debbie would be complete without a comment about her faith. She believes in her God, her church, and in the goodness of humankind. She is active in her church and participates when she can, but also states that a person doesn't need to attend church to be close to God. "Just pray," she smiles, "and He is with you."

On the D.A.W.N. website, Debbie was featured as the profile of the month (May 2002). The website may be reached at www.dawnser.home.mindspring.com.

Congenital Cataracts
A Life with Sight Impairment...

...Charles' Story

Incidences of congenital cataracts are rare, resulting in 4-5 births per 10,000 in the United States, although the rate internationally is probably much higher. While congenital cataracts are present at birth, they may not be identified until later in life. A cataract is an opacity (cloudiness) of the lens of the eye. If the cataract goes undetected at birth, permanent vision loss may ensue. The lens is located behind the pupil and focuses rays of light into the retina to allow image formation. The lens is able to change shape and can focus on objects at different distances. Its cells are arranged so that it is transparent, like glass or water. When this arrangement is disturbed in any way, the transparency is lost and an opacity results. This blocks or blurs the retinal image.

The most common causes are diseases of the mother, including hypoglycemia, Down Syndrome and infectious diseases such as rubella, chicken pox, syphilis and herpes simplex. Only about 20% of congenital cataracts are hereditary. Congenital cataracts can affect one eye or both. In bilateral (both eyes) cases the cataract may be denser in one eye and will develop vision differently.

Other disorders in the infant may also be present with congenital cataracts such as mental retardation, deafness, kidney disease and heart disease. Not all cataracts are visually significant and require removal, although many are. While the incidence of congenital cataracts is low, the effects can be crippling to a newborn. Most removals of the cataracts occur before the newborn is two months old. The delay in surgery is because of the possibility for developing glaucoma. The development of glaucoma (which occurs in later years) only occurs in eyes with cataracts that have undergone surgery. A delay of even a few weeks at birth allows the angle of the immature eye to develop.

Complications from congenital cataracts include loss of vision, even with aggressive surgery, glaucoma and retinal detachment. Removal of the cataract is only the beginning. Visual rehabilitation often requires years of refractive correction. If chromosomal or familial abnormalities are present, all offspring are at risk. The eventual outcome of a child born with congenital cataracts depends upon the type and severity of the cataract. Some impair vision to a small degree only and never require surgery. If the cataract is unilateral (one eye only) there is a strong tendency for the child to emphasize the healthy eye so that the eye affected by the cataract rarely achieves normal vision. Most prominent of the complications from any cataract is glaucoma.

Resources & Information

Gale Encyclopedia of Childhood & Adolescence,
    www.gale.com; 1-800-877-GALE
University of Utah, John A. Moran Eye Center, Salt
    Lake City; 801-581-2581
The Abilene Eye Institute
    www.abileneeyeinstitute.com
Healthlinkusa.com
BayInsider.com
Canadian Ophthalmology Society: www.eyesite.ca
National Library of Medicine: www.nlm.nih.gov
Spears & MacLeod Medical links:
    www.spearsmacleod.com
The Eye Care Connection: www.eyecarecontacts.com

Charles' Story
A Life with Sight Impairment...

...Congenital Cataracts

Starting a family is often the most wonderful experience a young couple can have. Filled with expectancy and wonder, life changes forever for the couple when the baby is born. For most parents, holding their perfectly formed child in their arms seconds after childbirth is a feeling unequal to any in the life experience. For some parents, however, the birth of a child is more traumatic, and much more painful.

Charles was born on a cold December morning in 1938 in Kansas City, Missouri. In those days, vision was not checked, so neither the doctors or his parents had the slightest inkling that something was wrong. It was discovered that he was tongue tied, but a quick surgical procedure corrected that. Tragically, seventeen days later his mother died from complications of childbirth. His dad was then faced with the responsibility of raising a baby while trying to eke out a living on a depression era farm in rural Missouri. On Mother's Day, 1939, he took Charles to his grandmother and said, "Mom, I just can't do it. Would you take him?" His grandmother had already raised four children and partly raised one grandchild, but she accepted the responsibility. A month later, a great aunt was giving Charles his bottle and realized that something was wrong. "This child is blind," she told Charles' grandmother. Things happened quickly after that. Over the next six months, Charles had four operations to pierce and partially remove the cataracts that were obscuring his vision. Another surgery at age five completed the job.

As Charles was tested in his first year or two of life, doctors were pessimistic about his chances for a normal life, but as he developed and grew, Charles began to surprise even the most pessimistic of the physicians about his ability for normal development. Charles did develop normal speech and was very verbal once he started talking. Doctors also predicted a learning disability, yet the young boy developed faster than other children his age, displaying much higher learning capacity than anticipated.

With the assistance of heavily refracted prescription lenses, young Charles looked forward to starting school, but his grandparents and doctor were skeptical. Would a child who was legally blind be able to function in public school? The decision was a difficult one, and Charles was even considered a candidate for a school for the blind. In the end, however, his grandmother insisted that he not be segregated from normal youngsters and they enrolled him in public school.

"I was teased," Charles says. "I wore thick glasses that made my eyes look large and kids laughed at me. It hurt, sure, it did."

It was the first time that he began to consider himself as a child who wasn't like other kids. Unlike some of the more cruel kids at school, his dad, grandparents and neighbors all treated Charles as they would any other child.

"I really didn't understand why they teased me at first," Charles admits. "I mean, I wasn't the only child who wore glasses."

For Charles, the blackboard was not easily seen. Any object in the distance was blurry and appeared to him as shapes only. Details were impossible to see, and because of this, Charles learned to listen well as the teacher wrote on the chalkboard and spoke to the students. He paid very close attention to what the teacher was saying as she wrote so he would not miss out on any instruction.

Charles loved to read, and from any early age he read voraciously. Unlike children with normal sight, book pages had to be held very close to his eyes for him to be able to see the words. He quips, "I always had a black nose from getting too close to the pages." His grandparents purchased a series of twenty volumes called *Books of Knowledge*. Every night after school and often on weekends, Charles read from these books. He read every word and every sentence and absorbed knowledge as a sponge absorbs water. Each volume was hundreds of pages, and they were his favorite reading. He also read most of the school library biographies and the entire *Tarzan* series by Edgar Rice Burroughs. "I was a very slow reader," Charles says, "but I retained almost everything I read. I just couldn't see the words very easily so it took me longer."

Few can imagine the enormous challenge that a legally blind child has in normal day-to-day activities. Charles could not read signs, nor could he see distant objects with any clarity. Many thought that riding a bicycle would be too dangerous, but Charles acquired an old bike in the seventh grade and rode it to and from school and around town all through high school. As an adult, he rode to and from work and still has a bicycle that he rides occasionally. According to Charles, "People would tell me I can't do something and I just had to prove them wrong by doing it."

Living in a small Missouri community was good for Charles. Classroom sizes were small as the population of his entire community was only about two hundred people. With twelve to fifteen students per class, Charles had the assistance he needed to not only learn at a normal pace, but in fact, he was extremely bright and excelled at most subjects. "All except math," Charles admits. "It wasn't my best subject."

He admits to being overprotected. "Although I really didn't understand what a 'handicap' was," Charles says, "I was told that I was handicapped, and so I assumed I was." Except for the occasional teasing he took, most of the citizens in his small town were accepting of Charles' disability. "I think there wasn't the bias against people with a disability like there is now," Charles states. "Everyone knew me around town and pretty much accepted me."

As far as the teasing went, Charles is fond of saying: "I could see better than many who teased me could. I could see the person, all they could see was the glasses."

As he grew older, Charles always surprised even the most ardent of skeptics about his abilities. His unique and good sense of humor kept him centered and able to stay outgoing rather than withdrawing into himself. He was friendly to everyone and while there were always a few who were not accepting of him, Charles learned somehow to treat everyone with respect and kindness.

At high school graduation Charles was honored as valedictorian of his class. He had proven many people wrong, having overcome tremendous challenges in his young life. He started college in Kansas City. Services for the Blind provided Charles with a tape recorder to tape lectures because it was difficult for him to take notes in class. While seeing the detail on overhead transparencies and chalkboards always presented a problem to him, teachers would provide him handouts of the same material so he could study them later. Although challenging because of his sight impairment, Charles found college very much to his liking.

"People with disabilities often develop other senses to a much higher level," Charles says. "While I had an obvious visual impairment, I had a stronger sense of hearing than most. It simply is training. From an early age I had learned to concentrate more on what the teachers were saying and therefore had a much better memory and capacity to recall what had been said."

After graduating from college, Charles embarked on a teaching career and served in several school districts. Those experiences in teaching taught

Charles some painful lessons about the public bias among employers toward persons with a disability.

"I would be interviewed along with other candidates and not get the job," Charles recalled several early experiences out of college. "It was very frustrating. Back then I would just be told, 'We don't think you can handle this job.' I would almost beg them to give me a chance."

Frustrated and angry, Charles knew he was being passed over because of his sight impairment. Some employers admitted that they were leery of workers' compensation claims he might make. Many just never responded after the initial interview.

Charles had always been persistent. He knew that he simply had to work harder to get what he wanted and deserved from life. As a secondary education teacher in English and science, he was eventually hired, and for a variety of reasons, eventually, was fired.

"I could deal with anything in the classroom. Sure the kids would get away with things, simply because I couldn't see them and observe what they were doing, but as far as teaching went, I did the job. I was a tough teacher." Maybe too tough for some and not tough enough for others, Charles had several positions that all led to his dismissal. Most of the dismissals were based on discipline issues – the kids simply took advantage of his disability and school administrations did not offer him the type of support they should have.

Frustrated with secondary education and trying just to establish a career and find a school district he could stay with, Charles taught in Colorado, Oklahoma and North Dakota before finally deciding to leave teaching for a new career. In the meantime, he had met and married the love of his life. Although his wife also had a disability, her sight was normal. Charles finally had a pair of eyes that he could count on to help him grade exams and see signs. The couple would eventually have two daughters.

Believing that he should get out of teaching Charles headed back to college and went on to get his master's degree at the University of Wisconsin Stout in vocational rehabilitation. Working with persons who had disabilities was something that Charles knew he could do very well from experience. His degree in assessment and evaluation gave Charles license to test each person's qualifications and ability to perform in certain employment positions.

Immediately upon graduation Charles was offered the assessment and evaluation counselor position of a sheltered workshop in Twin Falls, Idaho. There he worked with vocational rehabilitation referrals as well as private referrals from insurance companies for work assessment. He had a found a home in employment counseling, a rapidly growing field. It also was a career in which Charles' own disability was not considered a hazard or company liability for employment.

Over the next several years Charles worked as a vocational evaluator in Louisiana, Kansas, Ohio and Texas before joining the Charlotte Institute of Rehabilitation in Charlotte, North Carolina. Managed care was taking hold in the insurance industry and Charles worked in an outcome-based position with a company that specialized not only in serving persons with disabilities, but also hiring them.

In 1997, Charles joined Goodwill Industries of Central North Carolina in Greensboro where he continues to work today.

Charles relies on public transportation to get from home to work, as he has throughout his entire adult life, although his wife drives, which enables him to have normal vacations and recreation. He volunteers with Services for the Blind among other agencies and always has compassion for anyone with a disability that comes through his program.

"I immediately know the struggle that many people have had their whole life," Charles says. "I think it makes me a better evaluator and a stronger counselor because I have been where they are in life. Sometimes it isn't about the disability; it's about the prejudice that employers have about it. That's particularly sad. It's just not acceptable, and I'll do everything I can to educate and train employers as well as my clients."

Charles can be seen every lunch hour with a book in his hands. At the bus stop he reads as well. He not only reads, he writes. Charles is an accomplished short story writer and poet. He also loves to latch hook rugs, play computer games and is active in his religion of the Baha'i Faith.

A disability has not stopped Charles from major accomplishment in his life. It has not slowed his education or learning. It has not stopped him from enjoying a family, now with three grandchildren. He occasionally still feels the sting of prejudice and public bias toward persons with disabilities, but dismisses it quickly. "I wonder sometimes," Charles says, "who has the real disability... me, or them?"

Spinal Cord Injuries
Injury to the Cord of Life...

...Ed's Story

Every year in the United States 11,000 debilitating spinal cord injuries occur. The results are life changing. Those are the survivors. Many more probably die at the scene of their accident. The number of people in the United States who are alive today and who have a spinal cord injury (SCI) have been estimated to number over 200,000, according to the Spinal Cord Injury Information Network. These traumatic injuries are like few other disabilities in that life for these victims forever changes.

SCI primarily affects teens and young adults. Fifty-five percent of SCIs occur among persons in the 16-to-30 age group. The second largest percent age of SCIs occur among older adults, sixty years of age or older. Overall, over eighty percent of injuries involving SCI occur among males. This three-to-one male to female ratio speaks more of lifestyle choices and has changed little over the past several decades. Race seems to also be a deciding factor in SCIs. The vast majority of injuries occur among Caucasian males, although the number of documented African-American injuries is catching up. Twenty-five years ago, almost eighty percent of SCIs were Caucasian.

Today, the percentages have dropped to sixty percent, with African Americans making up most of the difference.

Motor vehicle crashes account for thirty-eight percent of spinal cord injuries. According to the SCI Information Network, the next largest contributor is acts of violence (primarily gunshot wounds), followed by falls and injuries related to recreational sporting activities. Interestingly, trends show motor vehicle SCI cases falling while injuries from acts of violence and falls have increased.

Quadriplegics (paralysis in all four limbs) comprise over fifty percent of SCI accidents. These are injuries to one of the eight cervical segments of the spinal cord. Average first-year expenses for a quadriplegic can range from $370,000 to $570,000, and can average over $100,000 in subsequent years (depending upon the extent of care). Almost sixty percent of quadriplegics are employed at the time of their injury, and while the rate of employment drops significantly, almost twenty-five percent are still employed ten years later.

For paraplegics (those having lost two limbs) the employment outlook is brighter. While comprising forty-six percent of SCIs, these injuries involve lesions in the thoracic, lumbar or sacral regions of the spinal cord. Average yearly expenses for an individual in the first year can range over $200,000 and $20,000 to $25,000 thereafter every year. By year ten, over thirty percent are still employed.

Today, almost ninety percent of all persons with SCI are sent to a private, non-institutionalized residence (in most cases, their own homes). The rest are discharged to nursing facilities. Overall average days in a hospital following their injury have decreased in recent years from a month to about two weeks. Similar downward trends in the rehab unit following hospitalization are also occurring. From an average of four months in the rehab center, the average stay has dropped to about a month and a half.

Lifetime costs for a quadriplegic that is twenty-five years old at the time of injury can exceed two million, while costs for a paraplegic range about $500,000. While renal failure was the most common cause of death a few years ago for quadriplegic and paraplegic persons, modern scientific advancements have increased life expectancy considerably.

Here is Ed's story.

Ed's Story
Spinal Cord Injuries...

...Injury to the Cord of Life

Ed grew up in a large family in rural South Carolina. From an early age he was in trouble, taking a certain amount of pride in being labeled a "bad kid." Ed's father was a mechanic and his mother stayed busy raising the children.

In school, Ed was bright but had little time for studies. He was popular, played football and always had several girlfriends. Many of his classmates sought him out for his infectious personality and soft-spoken nature, but Ed had little time for the majority of the kids who wished to be friends with him. He was restless by nature and just didn't care to sit still in class, finding himself in the principal's office far too often. By high school, Ed was busy working every evening on cars; one of the great loves in his life.

Ed spent a lot of time with his good friend Sam. They worked on cars, fished, cut classes together, and would often got in trouble. At home, Ed's parents argued regularly. There was "always trouble" at home, Ed remembers, and he spent as little time there as necessary. His father drank heavily and during those times would be hard on Ed and his siblings, often beating them for the smallest of infractions. His mother worked as housekeeper in addition to the multitude of chores she performed while raising a large family.

Ed quit school in his junior year of high school and would not return. While he was "street smart" Ed had no patience for school, preferring to work instead. He obtained work in factories near his hometown and as soon as could he moved out on his own. When he was nineteen, Ed moved to North Carolina, going to work for a furniture manufacturer. He drank hard and played even harder. Young, strong, employed and living away from home, Ed felt on top of the world: no curfews, no violent arguments at home, and no beatings. He was finally on his own.

The euphoria, however, would not last long.

In a single night, just after his twentieth birthday, Ed's life would be forever changed. After a payday, on a Friday evening, Ed headed for the bar after work and drank for several hours with friends. When the bar closed, he moved to a friend's home and drank through the rest of the night, well into the early-morning hours of Saturday. Ed kept drinking and partying all Saturday afternoon and into the evening. From one house to another, Ed partied through the night until early Sunday morning. It was 4:00 a.m. when he finally left for home.

"I remember finally leaving my friend's house," Ed says slowly. He wishes he could take that day back. He has wished it every day of his life since. After twenty-four hours of drinking, Ed just needed to sleep it off, but he didn't.

"I owned a 900-cc Kawasaki KZ," Ed says softly, looking away toward an empty wall. He left the house with no shirt or shoes on, only a pair of jeans, and stumbled to the bike. He tripped and fell and crawled on his knees to the bike. With a few kicks the bike turned over and Ed began his last ride.

The medical report on Ed's accident estimated his speed at 115 mph. Ed remembers hitting a pothole and breaking a shock, but the cause of the accident was simply listed as "driving while severely impaired." From where he lost control of his Kawasaki to where he landed was 116 feet away. At 115 miles per hour, Ed's body was a missile when it flew off the careening bike into the ditch.

He landed hard, rolling over and over. He heard bones break and blood gushed from his head, but when he could not feel his legs, Ed knew he was in real trouble. He would live to regret this drinking binge.

Ed had snapped his spinal cord between the tenth and eleventh vertebrae. He was lucky that another motorist had witnessed his crash and came to his aid, just moments later. It turned out that the motorist had followed Ed and was his cousin, who had been drinking at the same party. Ed suffered broken bones in his hip and legs, had massive internal injuries and had sustained severe trauma to the head, which was bleeding both internally and externally.

The early morning hour and his cousin's impairment delayed the ambulance's arrival. By the time EMT personnel reached Ed, his body was curled in a fetal position and he had lost almost one-third of his body's blood. It took the ambulance forty-five minutes to reach him. He hadn't lost consciousness the entire time. Medics who finally reached him couldn't imagine how he'd even survived the accident with his injuries and radioed that the victim would probably not survive the ride to the hospital in High Point.

"One inch lower," Ed recalls, "and I'd be a complete vegetable I was told." The truth was, Ed was just plain lucky to be alive. A fractured skull left part of Ed's brain on the highway. His back was broken, along with a hip and both legs. Internal injuries to his kidney and spleen presented the first challenge to emergency room physicians.

When Ed arrived at the hospital, his head was twice its normal size. He was breathing and alert, although doctors couldn't understand why. Physicians worked through the next day to save him while Ed slipped into a coma. He survived the first day, but his condition worsened as more injuries were discovered. Throughout the second day his condition continued to deteriorate. Ed's parents and family were called. No one expected him to live. But the twenty-year-old struggled on. His condition worsened through the third day and only life support kept his young body alive.

Ed's mother was told he probably wouldn't survive, but in the off chance that he would, he would certainly never be the same young man again. Trauma to the brain would change his life forever, his family was told. He would never speak again, probably have little or no cognitive skills and it was a certainty that Ed would never walk again, if he were even able to sit up on his own.

For days, Ed clung to life. Breathing tubes kept him alive and IV's fed him. While emergency surgery had repaired much of the damage to the spleen, the kidney would not function properly again because of the damage to it.

For seven weeks Ed lay in a coma. Within a few days, his parents had to return to work to support the rest of the family. Alone, Ed lay in intensive care. While friends came at first, they gradually stopped visiting him. Soon he was completely alone. Ed lost forty-five pounds during those seven weeks of unconsciousness. From a small frame of 135 pounds prior to his accident, Ed dropped to 90 pounds in two months.

After seven weeks, Ed awoke from his coma and lay staring at a white room, flat on his back. He had no idea where he was or how he had gotten there. Thoughts of his friends and job came back to him, but nothing in this place was familiar to him. Nurses and medical staff started to replay the last two months of his life for him, but it was Ed's mother who filled in all the pieces.

"I couldn't feel my legs," Ed remembers as he opened his eyes and gazed at a world two months older than he had last recalled. "Then my mother told me that I'd been in an accident, broken my spinal cord and had barely survived." Ed had no feeling from the waist down, nor could he speak and he had limited use of his arms and hands. As the news of the last two months was told to him, Ed lay in disbelief. His last recollection was leaving work and having drinks with friends. Then he was told that two months had passed and that he would never walk and probably would never speak again.

"I wanted to die," Ed says. "When I realized what I'd done to myself, I just wanted to die and end it."

Ed's mother was brutally honest. He had been so drunk he couldn't walk, much less operate a motorcycle. He was lucky he hadn't caused an accident involving another car and been responsible for others as well. As it was, Ed was reminded that he'd have to live with the consequences of that 24-hour drinking spree the rest of his life.

"When the full impact of my injuries hit me, I just wanted to die," he says. "I couldn't imagine living without speech or without the use of my legs. What use did life have if I had to live this way?"

The first time Ed remembered a physician coming to see him in the hospital, seven weeks had gone by since his accident.

"Will I walk again?" Ed scribbled out on a chalkboard. The answer he received was sobering, to say the least.

"You will never walk again," the physician told him. "If you do, it will have to be between you and God, because I can't repair what you've broken."

Ed pondered his words. "Between me and God. He can't repair what I've broken." These were difficult words to think about for a twenty-year-old who had his whole life before him. "Between me and God." Ed didn't even believe in God. How would that help him? He couldn't talk, could barely use his arms and his legs lay as though they weighed a thousand pounds each, and no matter how hard he concentrated, they would simply not move, not even the wiggle of a little toe.

Ed was in the hospital a year. He spent almost a second year in a vocational rehabilitation unit. While he received daily therapy, he could not recover the use of his legs, although he felt excruciating pain shooting through his limbs, they did not respond to his commands. However his speech slowly returned. The recovery was painfully slow. His family was busy and rarely had time to see him, and all of his former friends had long since abandoned him. Ed was left alone, alone with the thought of driving while drunk, and ending life, as he had known it, for the rest of his life.

His therapy sessions were two hours a day, and always painful. Speech therapists worked on his garbled sounds, while physical therapists tried to keep muscle tone and circulation in his weakening legs.

"I would lie awake at night and cry," Ed says with a melancholy that few people could ever understand. "I know I had done this to myself, but it didn't make it any easier to live with." He was suicidal at times and deeply depressed most of the time. Therapy was difficult and painful, and the lack of intelligent speech made communication frustrating and equally painful.

To keep him mobile, therapists taught Ed to sew. At first he was all thumbs, but over time, Ed became pretty good at sewing. However life was difficult for him. He had no feeling from the waist down, resulting in many bladder and bowel accidents, which only added to his humiliation.

"You learn to appreciate a kind nurse or nurse's aide," Ed would say.

When he was finally discharged, Ed was wheeled to the front door and released. Staff members hugged him and a few family members, including his mother, met him. He moved home for a short time, but family conflict drove Ed to seek a place of his own, bringing him back to North Carolina.

Life was difficult for Ed. Bound to a wheelchair, he felt the sting of prejudice deeply. Many would look at him in sympathy, others would laugh or poke fun of him. In either case, Ed felt less than whole and deeply shamed. It's the bane of many individuals with disabilities – few can accept them in a society where beauty is measured by slim waist size and strength by the appearance of a man's chest.

Ed sunk into a deep depression. He found himself drawn back to alcohol for solace. He embraced the cause of all of his pain once again and found that through alcohol he could forget, even for awhile, that he was disabled.

Ever so slowly, Ed brought himself back. He sought out counselors at vocational rehabilitation to help him become retrained so that he could work again. It had been several years since his accident and he had to return to work. It eroded his self-esteem and ate at his sense of worth. Eventually Ed met a woman and married her. Sheila had also sought assistance from vocational rehabilitation and the two met while in counseling together. Sheila was hearing impaired and Ed learned sign language so the couple could communicate better, but as he had learned, life is not easy for those who suffer from a disability.

Lack of mobility was the greatest problem Ed faced. Just getting from place to place required so much thought and time. Wheelchair accessibility (while mandated by law) was not the norm, but the exception with many retailers. Bus transportation was even more difficult and required special handling. While transportation was available for Ed much of the time with pre-appointed schedules, the transportation was not reliable, and Ed was often left sitting for hours at an outside bus station, often in inclement weather.

The reality that life depended upon so many others was difficult for Ed to accept. He depended on individuals to help him dress, use the restroom, get to work, go to the park and so many other daily functions that others take for granted. Although life was tedious and difficult in a wheelchair, the stares from people hurt the most. Worse still, Ed began to believe that his self-worth was somehow tied to the use of his legs, or the strength of his body.

Although Ed had not been close to his father, his dad saw Ed's predicament and fashioned a special hand control from which to operate a car. He even installed the apparatus inside Ed's car. The gift of his father's mechanical ability gave Ed the opportunity to drive again. The freedom gained from transportation was more than Ed could have ever imagined before his accident.

"You just learn to appreciate so much more," Ed says. "I mean, I never thought I would ever drive again, but here I am."

An appreciation of life, even with disability, is the message that Ed brings now to everyone who will listen to him. That appreciation for physical mobility spilled over into other areas of Ed's life as well, including a renewed religious life, making him a more positive, valuable member of society and less oriented to himself.

When Ed came to Goodwill, he came as a pretty broken young man, but over the months that followed, he discovered within himself a new resolve, and a growing confidence.

"I can't thank Goodwill enough for everything I received. They made things happen for me and I'm so appreciative." Ed's confidence grew, as did his smile. He had hope again.

Substance Abuse
A Long Road to Recovery...

...Theresa's Story

According to the National Household Survey on Drug Abuse in 1996, 14 million people over 15 years of age were consuming illegal drugs in the United States. With almost 5% of the population using drugs, the economic impact on health, crime, accidents, loss of work and family abuse is staggering. Worldwide, according to the United Nations, 180 million people are believed to be consuming illegal drugs.

The impact on children is equally significant. Of the 75 million children under the age of 18 in this country, over four million have chronic substance-using/abusing parents (all substances, including alcohol) who are in need of treatment.

Marijuana, cocaine and heroin are among the most widely used illicit drugs consumed in the world. According to the NHSDA survey nearly three million individuals in the U.S. alone have used heroin at least once in their lifetime. Over 600,000 people have used heroin in the past year. There are twice the number of African-American users than Caucasians and three times the number of male users over females, and heroin has become a strong temptation for the young. Studies show an alarming rise in heroin use among students from the eighth through twelve grades.

Marijuana use doubled from 1992 to 1996 for youths 18 and under, increasing from 3.4% of the total population to 7.1%. From 1996 until 2001, the rate has almost doubled again, going from 7.1 to 13.2% of children 18 or under having used marijuana during the survey year.

The economic impact on society from alcohol and drug abuse is staggering. The National Institute on Drug Abuse estimates that the cost to the U.S. society alone was over $300 billion in the year 2000. Healthcare service costs for alcohol-related problems has topped $20 billion and is over $10 billion annually for drug-related problems. This cost includes detoxification and rehabilitation centers as well as prevention, training and research expenditures. The actual cost of the drug rehabilitation is only the tip of the iceberg. The drug problem has much broader implications than just drug usage. The spread of infectious diseases, money laundering, corruption and the financing of insurgent or terrorist groups have put the entire world on notice.

While the statistics are troubling, the *World Drug Report 2000* breaks through the psychology of despair that has gripped a generation, and reports confidently that the drug problem is neither unstoppable nor irreversible. Progress has been most significant regarding the two main problem drugs, cocaine and heroin. At the global level these two drugs are responsible for most drug-related treatment demand, hospitalization, overdose, mortality, violence and the involvement of organized crime. Prevention and treatment interventions seem to have stemmed the tide dramatically in recent years, resulting in a 40 percent decline in overall drug consumption and a 70 percent decline in cocaine consumption in the United States in the past ten years.

Successful drug and alcohol treatment stories are more the norm than the exception now.

Here is Theresa's story.

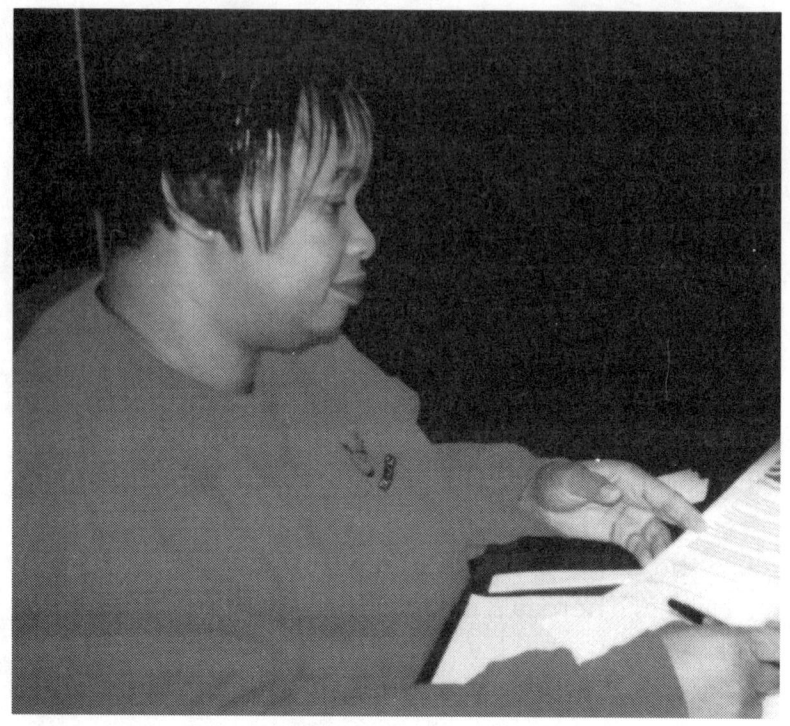

Theresa's Story
Substance Abuse...

...A Long Road to Recovery

Theresa is one the hardest working employees at the Greensboro regional office of Dun & Bradstreet. Voted by her coworkers as Best Motivator of the year in 2001, the award won her a complimentary vacation in Las Vegas. She also received the honor of being top sales producer, not of the regional office, but of the entire country for Dun & Bradstreet. Theresa's efforts within the organization also secured a grant award for Goodwill Industries from the national office of Dun & Bradstreet. This was a sizeable award to help build a new computer lab for the nonprofit agency.

Theresa is a model employee, however, this was not always the case.

Born in Brooklyn, Theresa's family moved to Philadelphia where she spent most of her young life. She grew up under the stern countenance and guiding hand of her mother and was always a hard worker and an achiever. As a teenager growing up in the seventies Theresa got caught up in the heavy undercurrent of the drug culture and abused not only cocaine but also became a heavy drinker, in an effort to fight her depression.

In 1987, Theresa became sober and returned some sanity to her troubled life. She married and had a son, Andrew, and rebuilt her life joining her mother as owners of a furniture store. From 1987 until 1996, Theresa was sober and free of drugs. She attended church, worked hard in the store, loved her husband and raised her son. She thought her drug-abusing days were behind her, blaming the past on youth and depression.

However life would change dramatically. In 1996, after her husband was awarded a sizeable settlement for being a victim in an auto accident, the family moved to Greensboro. There they purchased land and built a fine home. For Theresa it was a welcome departure from the congestion and size of Philadelphia. Greensboro was the home of her husband.

At that time of her life, the move to Greensboro would turn out not to be a good one for Theresa. Fighting recurring bouts of severe depression she started drinking again. It wasn't long before she started drinking heavily every day. The alcohol added to her depression. One night while at a party with new friends, Theresa accepted just one hit of crack cocaine. One was all it took to nearly destroy her life.

The weeks and months that followed were a blur to her. Theresa's self-destructive teenage lifestyle had returned quickly. She stayed high most of the time. At first, her husband supported her habit, spending money he'd earned from the settlement and working but by 1998, he was no longer able to support her escalating habit, a habit that had grown from a few dollars to over eight hundred dollars a day.

Theresa remembers calling her mother one morning after a night of binging. Her mother hardly recognized the voice. By 5:00 p.m. that same afternoon, her mother stood in Theresa's kitchen in Greensboro wondering what had happened to her daughter. "Theresa, you've turned from sugar to shit," she remarked. Theresa knew she was right.

Those who loved her reached out to her often, picking her up only to see her fall again. For Theresa, she lived from day to day, from one high to the next. She spent much of her time planning how she could get money again for more drugs. As Christmas of 1998 approached, Theresa didn't even bother with a tree or decorations. Arguments and painful disagreements had taken a heavy toll on her marriage, and her son withdrew deeper and deeper, causing him behavioral problems at school. As Christmas arrived, Theresa took her son and drove to Philadelphia to be with her mother. When it was time to leave her son Andrew clung to his grandmother and told his mom: "Grandma needs me here. I think I need to stay."

Theresa knew that even her son had had enough. When she returned to Greensboro, all responsibility in her life had ceased and her drug habit raged on. She turned to forging checks to obtain more and more drugs. When her husband couldn't cover them, the law stepped in with warrants.

The warrants led to jail time. At first it was for only a few days, but it gradually turned into weeks before her husband could obtain bail money to get her out. She tried to get sober abut Theresa couldn't shake her habit and was soon back in jail. She recalls one day when she was served a warrant in the morning, spent the day in jail, released in the late afternoon and was served another warrant in the early evening.

It was check forgery that landed in the Life Center for Drug Rehabilitation in Galax, Virginia for a month. Upon returning to her home, Theresa stayed sober for only a few weeks and was soon back doing drugs. She would do whatever was necessary to obtain drugs, stealing from her husband, pawning items they had purchased, and writing bad checks.

"I don't know why my husband didn't leave me," she recalls his extraordinary patience during that time. "He was a long-distance trucker and his time away from me was probably good for him. When he'd come home, he usually find me high or in some new legal trouble."

Theresa knew that her drug use would lead to ruin. Her mother couldn't reach her, nor could her husband. Even her son couldn't reach her. She was alone in her addiction and depression. She was utterly alone.

Early in 1999 Theresa was arrested again, this time for violation of probation. She knew that this time the charges meant prison and as she faced the judge and her case was read, tears welled from deep within her. They weren't tears of self-pity, but of remorse. She saw herself clearly that morning. When she heard the sentence it was as though the judge dropped a hammer onto her head. He simply said: "D.O.C.," meaning a three-to-five-year sentence at the department of corrections, or, state prison.

"The judge didn't even look at me. He just turned to the bailiff and said, 'D.O.C.' and I knew it was all over. I was so overwhelmed with regret and emotion I simply cried out, 'Lord, Lord, you promised me that

You wouldn't give me more than I could bear. Please!"

Her words surprised the judge. He looked at her for the first time, seeing remorse, pain and regret. "Okay, what do you have to say?" he responded to her. Theresa poured out her pain in those next few moments. "It's more than I can bear."

The judge was affected by her supplication and reduced the sentence that morning from 3-5 years to 14-18 months. Theresa says that her life began to change as they handcuffed her. Although Theresa will never forget the one-hour drive to the Raleigh State Women's Correctional Center and her first hours in that place, she reached deep within herself and resolved that she would straighten her life out. She had made so many promises to so many people before, but importantly, she believed that a higher power was beginning to work within her. It had started in the courtroom with the judge. She would reward his kindness to her.

"I always knew that God had a plan for me. I didn't think that this was a part of His plan for me, but maybe, just maybe it was." From the moment she stepped foot in the state prison for women in Raleigh, Theresa had a new mind-set. "I wasn't going to bring the same woman out that I had brought in."

Theresa made good on her promise to herself. She enrolled in a six-week drug program, known as D.A.R.T. within days of her arrival. Her determination and inner resolve impressed prison instructors. Theresa also connected with a prison ministry program and in time was recommended to attend the Mary Francis Center in Tarboro, a Christian drug and abuse center for women. Theresa attended the center by day, creating the opportunity for her to escape the negativity of daily prison life. At Mary Francis, Theresa took bible studies and began to seriously deal with her addiction, depression and life issues. Life at Mary Francis was exactly what Theresa needed. She found strength in the women there, and they found strength in her. Before her prison sentence was up, Theresa had started college classes and even volunteered outside of the center working for a food and clothing distribution location when waters from a hurricane overfilled riverbanks and flooded all of eastern North Carolina.

"I found purpose again," Theresa concludes. "I guess I needed prison to wake me up and help me see that life was sweet and good."

In June of 2000, Theresa went home. Her husband and son were waiting for her and welcomed her back with open arms. His loyalty brings tears to her eyes. "Women whose husbands go to jail rarely leave them," Theresa speaks of personal experience, "but the opposite isn't true very often. When women go to prison, most men leave. I am so fortunate."

Theresa left prison a different woman, just as she promised herself. She had found the peace and love of God while at Mary Francis. She had also recommitted to her family and especially, to her son. She had left alcohol and drugs behind. She knew exactly where drug use had led her in life and she vowed never to return to that hell. Her homecoming was sweet and filled with tears.

Theresa wasted no time in attempting to rebuild her life. While her spiritual life was solid, and her family reunited, Theresa needed a job. She feared that process the most. "I had heard that on every application there was a line that asked if you had ever been convicted of a felony. I also knew that most employers didn't want to mess with an ex-convict, so I realized that finding a good job was going to be difficult."

Theresa's life had turned serendipitous, however. She had a higher power guiding her now and believed that He would help find a way for her to work at a respectable and decent paying job. That's when Theresa found Goodwill Industries.

"I had heard that they had an excellent customer service training program at Goodwill, and I had $500, so I offered to pay them to take me as a student." Counselors at Goodwill told her that she didn't need to pay, that services were free to those who needed and requested them. Over the summer of 2000, Theresa attended the Goodwill Customer Service Training Program, followed by several weeks of intense computer training skills. "I guess I knew how to turn a computer on before attending classes at Goodwill, but that was about all."

One of the job counselors at Goodwill described Theresa as, "The model program participant. She worked diligently in class, accepted constructive criticism gracefully and treated everyone with the utmost respect."

While her days were spent training at Goodwill, Theresa enrolled in night classes at the technical college. She wasted no opportunity to learn. By fall, Theresa had graduated from the Goodwill training programs and was ready for a serious job search. She knew the obstacles she would undoubtedly face and she was ready to walk and knock on doors all day if she needed to. As regards the line on the application asking if she had ever been convicted of a felony, Goodwill counselors suggested that she simply answer yes, and write alongside of it, "will explain at the interview."

Theresa prayed for guidance. She prayed that God would lead her to a company that would hire her and into an environment where she could prove that she was trustworthy, loyal and hardworking. All she wanted was a chance.

"I read an ad for Kelly Services that they were hiring for customer service representatives for the telephone center at Dun & Bradstreet, so I went to Kelly to fill out the application," Theresa says. "When I got to the line on the application that asked if I'd ever been convicted, I simply checked it yes and wrote, 'will explain at interview.' " When she was interviewed, she was a bit surprised and delighted that she wasn't asked about her conviction and was sent over to interview with representatives at the Dun & Bradstreet call center. Realizing her worst fear, she was asked to fill out another application. Again she checked the box yes, and wrote, "will explain at interview." Almost miraculously, the interviewers at the company passed over the line and did not ask her about the conviction or her past and offered Theresa a job that same day.

"I was so excited! I was jumping up and down and shouting in my car! I couldn't wait to get home and tell my husband."

Theresa started her career with Dun & Bradstreet by being a model student in their training programs. They offered their model of success and Theresa adopted it, every detail of it. She practiced her presentation at home, over and over again, until she not only knew it by heart, but also could deliver it convincingly. She began as a telephone data consultant and after a few months was promoted. She became a model employee and a hard-working representative for the company.

"My employer never held my background against me," Theresa says. "I'm so grateful for that. I give them 100%, every moment of every day."

When the company holds training classes, Theresa can always be found in the front row. If her colleagues cut up and joke during class, Theresa simply moves. "I don't have time to waste with that sort of thing anymore. They hired me to do a job, and

I'm determined to not only do the job, but do it better than everyone else."

Doing it better is what Theresa has done. In her first year at Dun & Bradstreet, Theresa distinguished herself by leading the office in sales. Although she appreciated the honor, it wasn't enough for her. Recently, Theresa was honored as being the top sales representative in the entire company, nationwide.

Because of the change in her life, her son also received the attention he needed. She enrolled him in private school so that he would get the best education he could receive. He is now on the A-B honor roll and plays three team sports. "Andrew is a happy and popular boy now," Theresa smiles. She knew that he had it in him all the time, he just needed a chance to prove it.

"Some people are born with a handicap," Theresa says. "I saw them struggle every day when I was at Goodwill. But I did a really dumb thing and added a handicap that wasn't there and made my life difficult when it didn't have to be. I really messed up. I became a borrower, not a lender. Now I have a lot of catching up to do."

Theresa recently wrote and applied for a Dun & Bradstreet national grant that was awarded to Goodwill Industries. When the grant was received and the check was presented to Goodwill to add on to the nonprofit company's computer lab, Theresa was there, along with executives from Dun &

Bradstreet. The smile on her face said it all: Theresa had become a lender, not a borrower.

This is a very personal story that was shared with you as a testimony to the love that Our Father has for us. There is no situation that is too hard for Him for those that believe. I am sharing my story hoping to add a beacon of light to someone else's path in their time of darkness. Theresa Godfrey.

Women in Prison
Rebuilding a Life After Incarceration...

...Theresa's Story

Women comprise a small percent of incarcerated adults over eighteen. In the United States, approximately five-percent, or about 95,000 women, are in local, state or federal prisons. The majority are in prison for economic crimes. The most typical convictions resulting in imprisonment for women are property crimes, such as check forgery and illegal credit card use. Nearly half of all women in prison are currently serving a sentence for a nonviolent offense. Two-thirds of all female inmates had two or fewer prior convictions.

Of the women convicted of violent crimes, the vast majority were convicted for defending themselves or their children from abuse. Tragically, average prison terms are almost twice as long for killing husbands as for men who kill their wives.

Most of the female state prison inmates are over thirty, have graduated from high school or have a GED, and are members of a racial or ethnic minority. The Bureau of Justice Special Report on Women in Prison released recently revealed that ninety percent of women in prison are single mothers. Often these mothers lose contact with their children once imprisoned. Today there are over 200,000 children in the U.S. whose mothers are incarcerated.

In recent years the number of women being sentenced to prison terms has risen. During the past decade the number of women in prison has increased 138%. The exploding populations of inmates are largely drug offenders, but even the incidence of violent offenses is on the rise. Women are still more likely than men to serve time for a drug offense and less likely to have been sentenced for a violent crime. Sixty percent of women offenders grew up in a single-parent household, and more than half reported having siblings that also have served or are serving a sentence. Forty percent of women report being physically or sexually abused before incarceration. Nearly two-thirds of women serving a sentence for a violent crime had victimized a relative, intimate or someone else that they knew. Two-thirds of women inmates have at least one child younger than eighteen, but only nine-percent actually have been visited by their children while in prison.

According to a May 1997 report of the Women's Economic Agenda Project, "Racism and economic discrimination are inextricably linked to sexism in our culture, creating severe inequalities in the court system and the prison system. For example, black women are twice as likely to be convicted of killing their abusive husbands than are white women. Black women, on average, receive longer jail time and higher fines than do white women for the same crimes."

The rising rate of convictions and sentences for women is not thoroughly understood. It is possible that deteriorating economic conditions are now pushing women to the brink faster than for men; as the primary caretakers of children, women may be driven by poverty to engage in more "crimes" of survival.

Incarceration has severe and particular ramifications for women. With over eighty percent entering prisons as mothers, the pain of forced separation from their children makes imprisonment far more traumatic for women than for men. They are often the sole caretakers of their children and were the primary source of financial and emotional support. Their children are twice as likely to end up in foster care than are children of male prisoners. In surveys of imprisoned women, the pain of separation for mothers of their children is the greatest punishment of incarceration and engenders despondency, and deep feelings of guilt and anxiety about the welfare of their children.

Once discharged, women find employment in society more difficult to obtain. While employment is difficult for every felon, society's treatment of women who have been imprisoned is considered much harsher.

100 Years of Goodwill
Touching Lives Through the
Power of Work

*"Friends of Goodwill, be dissatisfied with your work
until every handicapped and unfortunate person
in your community has an opportunity to develop
to his fullest usefulness and enjoy a maximum of
abundant living."*

Edgar J. Helms

Goodwill Industries is about working people, and the value that work holds for everyone. For one hundred years, Goodwill Industries has been working quietly on behalf of individuals with disabilities and disadvantages to help them attain self-sufficiency through work. The number that this worldwide nonprofit agency have benefited directly in its one hundred years is staggering – nearly six million people.

Goodwill Industries believes that all work has dignity, and that work not only enhances individual dignity but also brings hope for a better future to the entire family. Goodwill believes that through work, people find purpose, honor, friendship and identity. It is work that builds up the backbone of society and builds strong families and strong communities.

This unique agency, made up of 187 separate agencies throughout America and in thirty-five nations in the world, places someone in a full-time job every two minutes of every business day. These individuals are often the most difficult to place and the most shunned by the economic workplace. For the disabled in America, unemployment is approximately seventy percent. Worldwide estimates range as high as eighty percent for unemployed individuals who are disabled. No other socio-economic group of individuals ranks higher in unemployment. Worldwide, almost 400 million people of working age have disabilities.

It is not just the disabled population that Goodwill Industries seeks to serve. Worldwide, over 1.2 billion people are below the poverty level. Another three billion people worldwide are looking for work or are not making enough money to rise out of poverty. Forty percent of the world's population falls into the gray area of living in impoverishment.

What are the roots of an agency so dedicated to employment and job training for persons with disabilities and disadvantages? How did it begin, and how has it evolved to serve so many in its first one hundred years of history?

Long before the world's modern governments ever considered social and economic programs for citizens with disabilities, there came a Methodist minister from Iowa. He embodied the belief that everyone should work for their daily bread, but that some

needed a hand up to find the work necessary to earn
the bread. He believed that there was a job for
everyone who wanted one. He also believed that every
individual alive, regardless of their disability, had
value.

From a single mission in Boston incorporated in
1902, Goodwill Industries has grown to be one the
world's largest nonprofit providers of employment
and training services for people with disabilities and
other disadvantaged conditions. Goodwill Industries
addresses such social conditions as welfare
dependency, illiteracy, criminal behavior and
homelessness. It has championed the rights of the
disabled and disadvantaged, returning self-
sufficiency and hope to almost six million individuals
and their families.

The idea of Goodwill began when Methodist
minister Edgar J. Helms developed a plan to provide
employment and job training for the poor in Boston.
Helms put needy men and women to work restoring
unwanted garments and other articles, giving them
the opportunity to learn trades, skills and modest
wages as they worked. This cycle of donations,
processing, resale and wages was the beginning of
Goodwill Industries and has remained essentially
intact through the years. Today Goodwill Industries
is a $1.9 billion set of nonprofit organizations that
provide a chance for people impeded by
socioeconomic barriers to reestablish themselves in
society with dignity and hope. The concept that

Helms developed at Morgan Chapel in Boston's South End has been applied in 187 cities domestically. Each Goodwill organization operates as an independent nonprofit agency, providing vocational training and supportive services to individuals with barriers to employment. A national office comprised of support staff and visionaries offers continual services to the independent Goodwill organizations.

Helms was born on January 19, 1863 in a lumber camp near the wilderness town of Malone, New York, just south of the Canadian border. His father, William Helms, was logging crew superintendent and his mother, Lerona, was camp cook. Young Helms and his siblings were looked after not only by their parents, but men and women of the camp all pitched in to support one another.

In 1865, when Helms was only two his parents took advantage of the 1862 Homestead Act, and the family moved to Nashua, Iowa. In this small, rural, Midwestern town, Helms grew and went to school. From an early age, his mother knew that her son Edgar had been selected for an important purpose in life. She shared much of her vision with her son, who, in 1878, at age fifteen, became a printer's apprentice at the *Beacon*, the local newspaper in Nashua. Although his mother saw a different vision for her son, Helms began what he hoped would be a journalistic career. The newspaper staff quickly saw that young Helms had more talent than winding paper through a printer. He possessed an ability to write and had a passion for causes. After working as an apprentice, Helms earned a spot as a reporter, covering general stories for the paper, but his favorites were human features. Helms might have stayed working as a local community newspaper reporter, but felt the call to move on and attend college. Reluctantly he left the *Beacon* after three years to attend Cornell College, a respected Methodist institution in Mount Vernon, Iowa.

The William Sands Helms family in the 1870s – Standing are Edgar James and Mary Alzina. Seated (left to right): William Wallace, Lerona Sherwin Helms, Eda Estelle and William Sands Helms. (Photo from "The Ancestors and Descendants of Williams Sands Helms.")

Because of his limited funds, Helms worked numerous hours in addition to his full-time studies, making college life difficult and trying. He left college in the spring term of his third year and went back to work for the newspaper. Over the next four years Helms and his partner Edward Blackert purchased and published two newspapers. Before he was twenty-one, Helms' strong temperance editorials and solid journalistic style led to his selection as chairman of the Clay County, Iowa, delegation to the state Republican convention where a prohibition platform was adopted. At the state political convention Helms was captivated by the energy of political science, and appalled at the poorly informed and unqualified candidates among those running to represent their constituencies.

Feeling the power given by the people only through voting Helms led a successful county campaign to unseat "a rum candidate for legislature." Although he ran a spirited campaign, Helms was unsuccessful in his bid for public office; his experiences ultimately led him back to Cornell to finish college and ultimately, into a life as a minister and a missionary. He sold both his newspapers and used these funds to support his final year in Cornell, graduating in 1889, and later attended Boston University's Theological School.

In 1892, Helms married his longtime fiancée, Jean Preston, who had joined him in Boston at the

Theological School for deaconess training. The two began devoting much of their spare time providing missionary support to the immigrant, mostly Italian population, in the North End of Boston. Although the couple had dreamed of moving to India to continue their missionary work, lack of funds forced them to remain in Boston. At the age of thirty-two, in 1895, the district office of the Methodist Church offered Helms the ministry post at Morgan Chapel, in Boston's, mostly Irish, South End. The church had been started in the same location years earlier by Henry Morgan, an inner-city minister with a tough facade who often used food to entice the many wayward souls of Boston's South End to his chapel. Here, at a dilapidated inner city mission is where Helms vision of Goodwill began.

Years later, in his memoirs, Helms reflected on his decision to enter the ministry and the inner conflict he felt, torn between a career in business or a service to others through the church.

"From my earliest recollection I felt 'called' to preach. I have no doubt I received that call from my mother and the Almighty before I was born. Yet for years, I was disobedient to the heavenly vision. I was ambitious to be famous. I wanted to escape the privations of the frontier minister's lot. The hardships and precarious provisions of pioneer preachers did not set me so greatly against taking up the work of a minister as my ambition to become a 'great man.' My spirit always rose to a difficult task,

A young Edgar J. Helms began a career in newspaper publishing but felt he was "called to the ministry." (Photo from "The Ancestors and Descendants of Williams Sands Helms.")

and I instinctively knew 'God would provide' if I should preach. But I could not shake the ambition for fame. I saw no chance of that in the ministry. Moreover, I felt that to desire fame was unworthy of the minister's calling."

From the outset of his work at Morgan, Helms was focused on using the church to meet community needs. Under Helms' supervision, the chapel provided solutions for bathing and laundry services, created a children's center, a nursery, kindergarten, and led the effort against local prostitution and underworld elements in his parish. In the fall of 1896, Helms added an industrial school and night school, and in 1897, a school of music.

In his writing, Helms recalled his early days at Morgan Chapel.

"In the South End I was asked to take charge of one of the most unique religious missions ever founded. The founder was Henry Morgan, a tall, gaunt Connecticut Yankee who was said by his friends to look like Abraham Lincoln. The South End of Boston was fast becoming a segregated district for licentiousness, gambling and many other forms of vice. I went into the most vicious neighborhood I have ever known. The police were in league with the keepers of vile resorts and it was perilous to traverse the streets day or night."

Before his death from tuberculosis, Henry Morgan brought men and women to the mission by serving them a breakfast while he took the opportunity to preach to them. Helms changed the free-meal approach when he took over the Morgan Chapel. "Some accused me of lacking sympathy," Helms would write, "But it was not a lack of interest in the man who had lost his way, it was a change of emphasis and method I was after." From his earliest days in the ministry Helms believed in offering not charity, but a chance.

In the book *The Golden Threads of Destiny,* by Frederick C. Moore, who was a 55-year member of the Morgan Chapel and personal friend of Helms, he wrote: "Dr. Helms never seemed to take time to have proper rest. He was always on the go, day and night. After he became known in the neighborhood, persons were calling upon him, bringing their problems to him seeking information and help. He had a way of meeting folks so that even though at times, he was not able to do very much for them, somehow these people went away relieved because they found someone who would listen to them and had an interest in helping them to solve their problems."

Within his first few years at Morgan Chapel Helms had opened a night school to teach carpentry, cobbling, printing, tailoring, dressmaking and millinery. He believed that unemployed workers didn't just need a meal, but a job. He offered the training to individuals who could not get into other schools to learn a trade and charged them nothing. During the industrial depression at the turn of the century people who were out of work and looking for jobs crowded this school.

Those close to Edgar Helms were often surprised at his depth of character and fervent desire to make a difference in the lives of everyone around him. Frederick Moore said of the minister from Iowa:

Morgan Memorial Chapel, the birthplace of Goodwill.
(Photo from Morgan Memorial Goodwill Industries, Inc.)

The doors of Morgan Memorial Goodwill Industries were always open, no matter what the time of day, no matter what the need. (From "The House of Goodwill," Morgan Memorial Press, 1925.)

"I find that it is just about impossible for me to give a real description of E.J. Helms. No matter how closely one may have been connected with him, one was continually surprised with new glimpses of his personality and character. For me, it was a rich experience to know him."

Helms was a man who believed very thoroughly in prayer, and often solved the most pressing problems in his life and church by gathering his workers together and praying about the matter. Moore recalls that this time of prayer and contemplation was important to Helms saying, "This was a great help to the doctor because his tendency was to jump very quickly at an idea. The doctor even admits that had he not taken time to pray and think on matters, many mistakes would have been made."

In 1899, his wife Jean, after tending to others with tuberculosis, contracted the disease herself and died later that year. At about the same time, Helms learned that the city was preparing to condemn the Morgan Chapel building as unsafe and have it torn down by the spring of 1900. Distraught over the condition of the church, Helms gathered his staff together to pray and contemplate their future. Undaunted by what seemed to be imminent total destruction of his church and grounds, Helms moved his staff and missionary operations by renting other nearby facilities until he could secure a mortgage and proper funding for a new facility.

The earliest beginnings of Goodwill Industries at the Morgan Chapel saw people flock to the chapel asking for help. Ministers of various churches began to learn of the work that Helms was attempting to do in the South End, and he was invited to go to some of their churches and clubs to tell about the work and the plans which he had for the future. Because of these talks of the need of these people, packages of clothing, etc. were being sent in, sorted and put into what was called a 'Relief Closet.' As word spread of the closet, chapel workers began to be overrun with individuals coming out of great need.

Frederick C. Moore, a Boston business executive at Thomas Wood & Co., wholesale coffee and teas, devoted much of his spare time to volunteering at Morgan Memorial Goodwill Industries. (Photo courtesy of Morgan Memorial Goodwill Industries, Inc.)

Helms was concerned about giving items away for free, believing that he was "encouraging people to accept charity, rather than building up some kind of self-reliance." Contemplating the issue, Helms called the leaders of the chapel and his staff together one evening and said, "we need to find a way in which we can help these folks to help themselves." He also challenged his staff to assist him with a concept that would allow them to be charitable, yet allowing people a chance to become self-sufficient.

In the days that followed, Helms formulated the concept of an employment bureau. He appointed Mary French, a missionary who had recently returned from India and a member of the Morgan Chapel, to head up the bureau. It became her job to find employment for as many individuals as she could. The first Employment and Welfare Bureau was started in connection with the relief efforts at the church. "Of course," Moore wrote, "At that time Dr. Helms did not realize that the pattern was being woven that would spread all over America."

While the employment bureau seemed to be an excellent idea, jobs were scarce in Boston's South End. Helms ended up employing many of those seeking a job by making the donations more serviceable, particularly with furniture, shoes and clothing. As clothing donations increased, it became apparent that some or much of the clothing needed cutting or repair to fit children in need. Through that need, the employment bureau staff began to hire women who could do this kind of work, offering wages. Once the industrial depression had passed, a lot of competent workers found work, but Helms was challenged with the job of finding positions for the old, handicapped or injured people who could not be easily placed.

The issue arose quickly of how Helms could raise the money to sustain his employment bureau. Helms and the coffers of the chapel were nearly broke and faced the destruction of his mission if he could not find a way to raise money. He pondered his growing dilemma, praying fervently for a solution. He challenged his staff daily to help him find the answer that he believed was not far from his grasp.

Moore recalls the day that he stood with Helms when a woman appealed to the pastor for a coat for her little girl. She addressed the pastor saying, "Dr. Helms, I don't want you to give me this coat. I have very little money, but I don't like to receive charity. I will be glad to give you fifty cents for the coat. I wouldn't want it given to me." Helms was so touched by the woman's sincerity that he took the fifty cents and gave her the coat.

Those close to him saw Helms' face light like a candle in a dark room. The answer to his prayers had presented itself in the form of a woman who was willing to pay fifty cents for a coat that had been repaired by one of his workers.

"Mr. Moore, I have an idea," Helms told his friend. "After these goods are sufficiently repaired, we will have a sale once a week at the church. These goods could be sold at reasonable prices so that some of the folks could afford to purchase certain articles." So, a small office in the rundown old Morgan Chapel was turned into a sales room once a week for the public to shop and purchase goods. The staff at Morgan passed out leaflets advertising the clothes and household items that were for sale in the "Relief Closet." Helm's concept was to sell these donated items at a price that everyone could afford, thus recycling clothing and other items that one family could no longer use to a family that needed these items.

The first week of the advertised sale found people standing in long lines waiting for the doors of the Relief Closet to open. Helms stood behind the counter with his office staff and watched with glee as his small room was filled with women, men and children. Within a few weeks, Helms added a second shopping day at the chapel, then a third. Finally, he opened the small store every day of the week, except on Sunday.

Moore recalls another conversation with Helms as the novel idea of collecting donations from the more affluent families of Boston, repairing those collected items to provide some employment for individuals and reselling the items for a reasonable price, began to catch on.

"One day Dr. Helms said to me: 'Moore, we ought to have some way of collecting this material which the churches and housewives are saving for us. I have been thinking somewhat of perhaps getting some good clean sugar barrels, and have them put in the basements of the churches and club rooms, and then when they are filled, they could send them in by express.' I concurred with Dr. Helms that it was a good idea and told him that I could find him the barrels within the coffee business in town. I'm sure Dr. Helms already expected me to find them, even before I offered."

Moore located the barrels and bought twenty of them at a wholesale price. On the outside of the barrels was stenciled, "Morgan Chapel Industrial Relief Work." For the next few years, this is the method that Helms used for collecting materials in neighboring churches and service clubs in Boston. When the barrels were full, a horse-drawn wagon went to pick up the items and return them to the Relief Closet for sale.

As the amount of collected items from churches grew larger and larger, Helms brought his staff together and told them that he had heard of a junkman who was placing bags in individual homes, having his name on the bag, and then he would call and purchase the contents. "With brightness in his eyes," Moore wrote, "Dr. Helms says to us: Wouldn't the bag idea be just what we could use, except, of course, that we would not purchase the goods!'"

Helms believed in the goodness of his neighbors and fellowman. Although the junk dealer paid for the goods they collected, Helms believed that if wealthier families knew about the work of Morgan Chapel staff in attempting to find employment for men and women, that they would bypass the junk dealers and give the unwanted items in their homes to him.

The industrial relief effort at Morgan Chapel began to import burlap bags from South America. Thomas Wood & Company, provided the first thousand bags, and later, Mr. Rich of Chase & Sanborn Company began to donate thousands of bags to Helms' relief effort. The concept of modern Goodwill Industries had been born.

With burlap sacks in hand, Helms and his workers walked up and down the wealthier neighborhoods of Boston and asked for cast-off shoes, clothing, and virtually anything that they could carry away. Helms printed a pamphlet describing the work at Morgan Chapel and employed men to distribute the empty bags at the doorstep of these households. He also instructed the household to simply put the full bag on the doorstep and the items would be picked up.

Moore wrote: "One day the person in charge of our Bag Department called me, very much excited, and said, 'Mr. Moore, I have found a bag that you would like to see.' She brought it to my office and, believe it or not, she had in her hands, one of the first Goodwill bags placed in America! Stenciled on the burlap bag was the imprint: 'Morgan Chapel Co-Operative Industrial Relief Work' in a circular stencil

Coffee bags served as the first collection bags for "Morgan Chapel Industrial Relief Work." Thomas Wood & Company donated the first thousand burlap bags. Later, Chase & Sanborn Company donated many thousands of bags. (Photo from Morgan Memorial Goodwill Industries, Inc.)

125

with the initial IHN in the center. IHN stood for 'In His Name.' "

Edgar Helms probably never realized at the time that within fifty years, more than 2,812,707 Goodwill bags would be scattered over America, and that $12,000,000 would be distributed in the various Goodwill Industries to handicapped persons who were given employment by sorting the contents of these bags.

Helms employed individuals to distribute and pick up the bags on a routine basis. Wagons from Morgan Chapel began to be a routine sight within affluent neighborhoods of Boston. He also put men and women to work unloading, sorting, cleaning and repairing the collected items. When the items were ready to be sold, they were put in the relief closet and sold to the public for modest amounts. Women were employed to sew and repair clothing, while men repaired furniture, painted old items to restore their condition, and cobbled shoes for resale. Almost every item was considered usable. Helms believed that what was waste to one man was usable to another.

Helms noted that the poor retained a large measure of their self-respect and dignity if they were required to pay even a token amount for items offered in his retail store, but he never turned away the truly needy. Keeping true to his concept that Morgan Chapel was a mission for everyone, he used the generosity of the wealthy to clothe the poor, even if they did not have even a few coins with which to purchase the items.

The greatest problem Helms had in his new operation was informing the public about the work opportunities he had created at Morgan Chapel. He wrote pamphlets to housewives, letters to businesses, clubs and other churches, and spoke throughout the city to whoever would invite him. In one such letter, written in 1902, Helms informs his suppliers of a new service he is beginning to offer:

Dear Friends,

To find temporary work for the unemployed who apply to us during the winter months is one of our hardest problems.

You will notice by the enclosed report that during the past year we have done considerable along this line, but hundreds in distress have been turned away because we could find nothing for them to do.

To further develop this cooperative feature of our work, we are about to start a Salvage Plant, where we intend to use up all kinds of waste, such as paper of all kinds, old books, old magazines, rags, carpets, furniture, and metal. In fact almost everything can be used to good advantage. We expect to have teams to collect these things from our friends.

With sufficient patronage we can make this work self-supporting from the start and give aid to hundreds of worthy persons in the hour of great need by giving them a chance to earn what they get.

Their self-respect is maintained when we are able to keep them from becoming objects of charity. We do not employ the drunken hobo, only the man who wants to help his family and do right. In order to carry out this plan we invite your hearty cooperation. We must at once reach the kind-hearted, well-to-do people who give us their waste instead of selling it to the junk dealers.

It would be a great favor to us if you would mail us as soon as possible a printed list of your church or club membership. Thanking you in advance for your kind interest in the matter,

I remain,
Sincerely yours,
E.J. Helms

Helms had borrowed money to build a new chapel on the site where the original church had been destroyed in the spring of 1900. He also rented several nearby buildings to house his growing industrial services and employment bureau. He named his new church after the old, The Morgan Memorial Chapel. The great financial collapse of 1902-1903, however, created widespread unemployment among the poor of this area and caused the already poor population to become even more destitute and reduce many of the middle class to borderline poverty. For a time, Helms was able to support people by seeking donations from the more

Drawing of an early Morgan Memorial Goodwill Industries "relief bag" for donations.

affluent sections of Boston, however this method of fund-raising was not sustainable. Finances of the chapel fell on hard times and Helms struggled to pay the mortgage. His struggle to keep workers and staff paid while continuing to pay on the mortgage would continue for several years. The relief effort was working however, and growing by leaps and bounds.

By 1905, the relief work, now bringing collected goods by horse-drawn wagon, had grown to such a volume that Helms incorporated these efforts into an organization known as the "Morgan Memorial Cooperative Industries and Stores, Inc." These stores were run as a nonprofit, charitable corporation. The corporation operated not only in his church building but also expanded into several adjacent houses. Still Helms struggled financially with his own rapid growth.

In 1907, Helms formed the Morgan Memorial School of Applied Christianity, which taught courses and forums for youth and adult education. Ten years later this school would be absorbed by the Deaconess Training School, which was merged with Boston University in 1917 to become its School of Religious Education and Social Work.

By 1910, however, Helm's organization was in a dire state. Morgan Memorial Cooperative Industries, now formally incorporated, was facing financial disaster when the chapel's financial struggles continued. Helm's couldn't pay the mortgage note

A woman with polio repairs and dresses dolls for resale at the Morgan Memorial Goodwill Industries. (Photo from Morgan Memorial Goodwill Industries, Inc.)

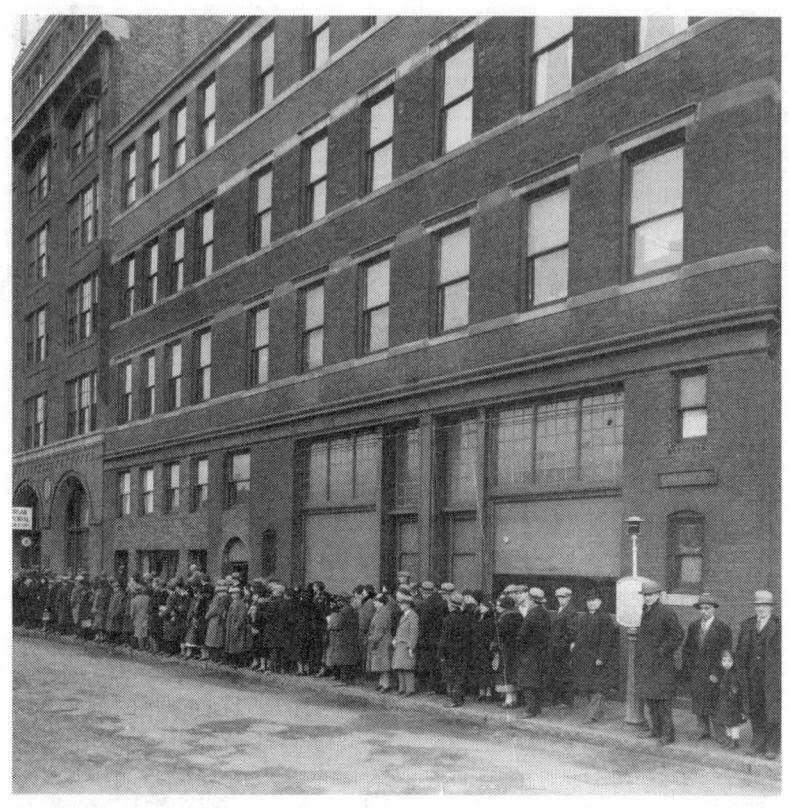

Hundreds of people in Boston's South End lined up each day at Morgan Memorial Goodwill Industries to receive help from this community-based organization. (Photo from Morgan-Memorial Goodwill Industries, Inc.)

and the bank sought to foreclose. Helms was using the proceeds of the sale of donated items to employ individuals, but his young corporation was struggling to meet expenses and pay on the debt of the building.

"I said to Dr. Helms when the auctioneer's flag was put up on the building," Frederick Moore wrote, "Is it possible that all of this work that you have started is to be closed out? Suppose someone comes to buy the building today, only to destroy it, would that be the end of it? He said to me, 'Moore, we are trying to be servants of God. We have worked out a plan. If someone comes and buys this building, then the plan in this place cannot go on, and somewhere, somehow, other fields of service will be opened. But,' he said, 'As you know, we have been praying a lot about this, and somehow I believe that things will come out all right.'

Helms brought his workers and church membership together and someone suggested that they sing that old 'Foundation' hymn and they all sang the second verse:

'Fear not, I am with thee, Oh be not dismayed, for I am thy God, and will still give thee aid. I'll strengthen thee, help thee, and cause thee to stand, upheld by my righteous, omnipotent hand.'

With such assurance and faith, it did seem as though prayers would be answered!

The bank's auctioneer came, and workers gathered in the little office at the front of the building. The auctioneer made his talk, but no one came to buy. Morgan Memorial had a reprieve. Helms immediately rallied other churches and institutions to assist in his fund-raising efforts. There was $40,000 to be raised. Helms' appeal was strong and urgent. He personally went from institution to institution looking for donors. In the end, even the bank that was to auction the building donated $10,000. Within six months Helms and his staff raised the $40,000 and were able to retain the buildings and property.

At the mortgage burning ceremony, Helms thanked everyone and closed by saying, "From now on, we pay as we go!" That became the slogan of life at the Morgan Chapel and found its way as a hallmark of the earliest days of the Goodwill movement.

Moore wrote of his experience as a fund-raiser for Helms. "That was my first experience in attempting to raise money. I remember very well when Dr. Helms gave me the name of a businessman, asking me to go and see him to ask for a donation for the building. I certainly did not want to let Dr. Helms down, for he was certain that the man would give. I was not so certain of course. I went down to his office, but passed by the door several times before I dared to go in. Finally, with the vision of Dr. Helms' conviction firmly planted in my mind, I knocked on the door and went in. He gave a substantial donation and I was elated to return to the chapel and tell Dr. Helms of it. It was as though Dr. Helms expected it, but thanked me cordially."

The buildings took care of the church work, also the Children's Settlement. In back of the Morgan Memorial was a court, called 'Osborn Place.' There were six buildings in this court, and it had the reputation of being one of the worst places in the South End of Boston. Open vice was carried on in all of the buildings.

This, of course, was a great annoyance to Helms and his workers. Helms set out to find the owners of the buildings in Osborn Place and was surprised to find that all of the buildings were owned by people outside of Boston who had no knowledge of the vice that was going on inside the buildings. Dr. Helms contacted the owner of one of the worst buildings in the court, No. 7, and found a woman by the name of Mrs. Whittemore of Providence, Rhode Island, to be the owner. He wrote a letter to her, to which he immediately received an astonished reply, saying that she did not know why Helms had written her such a letter. She said that she had never received complaints from the police and that the rents had always been paid. In the letter to Helms, she wrote, "You must be mistaken," but that she would personally drive to Boston and look into the matter.

When the landlord came to meet Helms, she was taken to the building she owned and after knocking at the door was greeted by an intoxicated man who swore at them and told them to go away. Mrs. Whittemore reportedly got into the man's face and told him, "I am the landlord!" She called up her agent

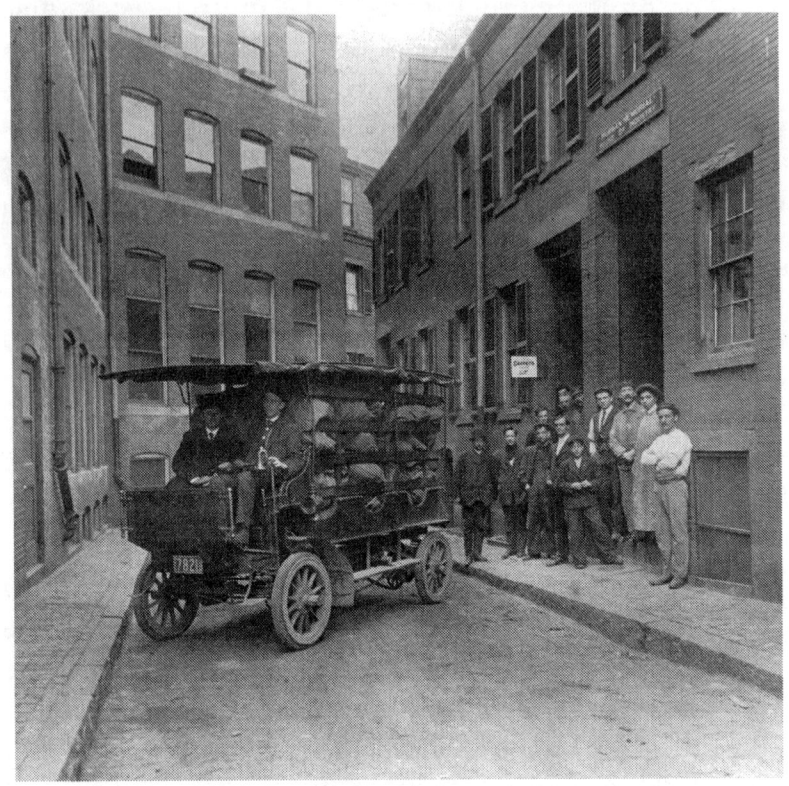

A collection wagon outside Boston's Morgan Memorial Chapel. Pictured at far right is Brother Thomas F. Benbury, an African-American minister and friend of Edgar J. Helms. (Photo from Morgan Memorial Goodwill Industries, Inc.)

and told him to send the keys to the building to Dr. Helms and the chapel, who would "personally look after the property from that day forward."

Hannah Parker Kimball, who bought the home for the purpose of donating it to Morgan Memorial, later

A fleet of donation trucks at Morgan Memorial Goodwill Industries. (Photo from Morgan Memorial Goodwill Industries, Inc.)

purchased the house. It was repaired, painted and furnished for workers of the relief effort. From that time forward No.7 Osborn Place became known as

"The House of Peace". In time, it became a home for children's, a striking transformation from earlier days.

The transformation of Osborn Place and the surroundings of the Morgan Chapel became a successful mission of Edgar Helms, whose spirit of overcoming obstacles Goodwill Industries would embody.

Helms' had a penchant for outdoor meetings in front of unsavory locations. One such location near the Morgan Chapel was Murphy's Saloon on the corner of Wheeler Street and Shawmut Avenue. A favorite story of Murphy's Saloon was told about one man who frequented the bar and staggered somewhat intoxicated from the place to hear Helms addressing a crowd out front, on the street. He followed the crowd for an after-meeting in the building at No.7 Osborn Place. Once inside, the man felt compelled to tell his story. He lived in South Boston. His boy was very ill. The doctor had ordered medicine for the youngster. Having no one else to send, the man's wife gave him money and told him to go to the drugstore for the medicine, warning him that the boy was gravely ill and that *he must* spend the money for the medicine. But before he could reach the drugstore, he passed a saloon, went in and spent the money. After drinking the liquor, he was so concerned about what he had done, and that his son might die, that he determined to throw himself over the bridge and end it all; but he did not seem to have

Dedication

of the

Morgan Memorial

Children's Settlement

Shawmut Ave. and Corning St., Boston

Sunday, March 1, 1914

3 O'clock

A pamphlet to announce the dedication of the Morgan Memorial Children's Settlement, March 1, 1914.

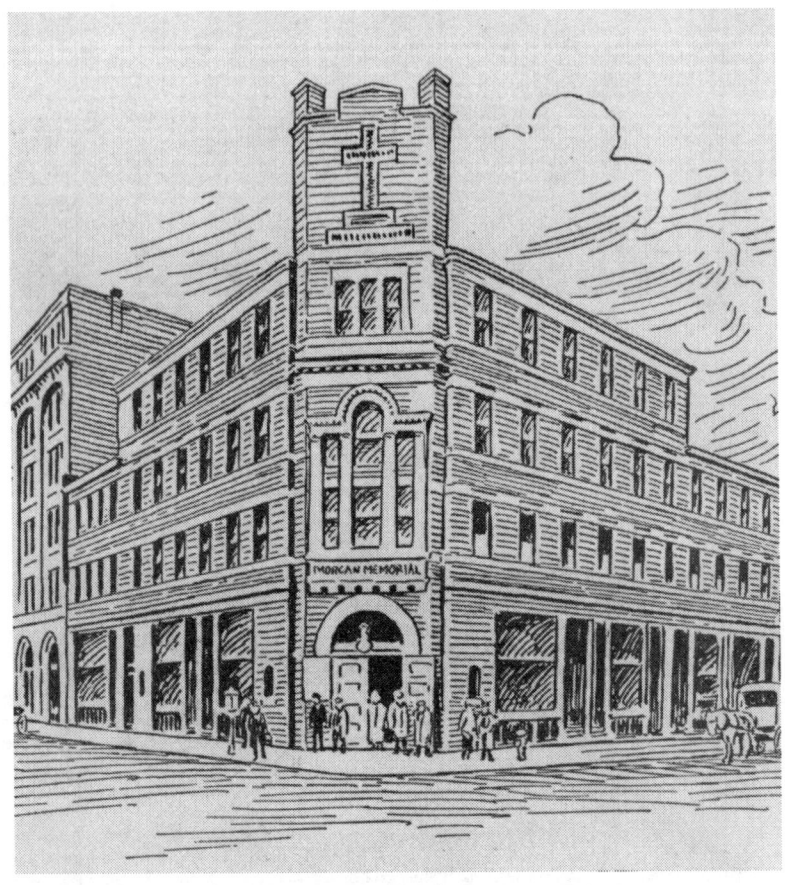

Drawing of the Children's Settlement and Industrial Plan, Morgan Memorial.

an opportunity because of a passerby. Then he heard the singing and came to the meeting.

After listening to his story, a worker from the Chapel went with him and bought the medicine and visited the home. The drunken man was so touched and affected by what the other man had done, that he signed a pledge and said that he would never drink again. The relief worker found the family was living under very bad conditions and arranged for the family to move to No. 8 Osborn Place recently purchased by Helms. This man became interested in the religious work and worked at Morgan Memorial for a while. Later he secured a good position in New York, having stuck to his promise to quit drinking. In his later years he visited the mission and Helms learned that his boy was studying for the ministry.

The creed of the early efforts at Morgan Memorial became: save *material waste and turn it into human well being.*

Another story concerning Osborn Place and the transformation of lives that was taking place because of the work of Edgar Helms has been passed down through the years and once again, recorded by Moore.

The Maltese cross symbol used by Goodwill Industries of America from the early 1920s to the 1950s.

141

MILWAUKEE EDITION   VOL. 2.   MARCH, APRIL, MAY, 1924 No. 3.

NOT CHARITY, BUT A CHANCE!

"Not Charity, But a Chance!" one of the many phrases used through the years to describe Goodwill's work in providing employment opportunities rather than charity.

Helms was Chaplain of the Charles Street Jail for a number of years. There he met a man by the name of DeLeRue. Mr. DeLeRue had been somewhat addicted to drink, but also had used drugs. There was scarcely anything left of him but a skeleton. He was nervous, underfed and suffered from other maladies. Helms asked the man to come to one of the workshops and found that he knew a good deal about painting so gave him some work in the paint shop. As he worked there, he became interested in the chapel service and attended the meetings. Many times he would state that it was only because of the fact God was helping him, that he could overcome the temptation, particularly concerning drugs.

He often spoke of his wife and daughter whom he had not seen for 17 years. The last time he had seen them was in a city in the Midwest. He had lost track of them. After he had been with them a while, he asked that the church employees might pray that somehow he might get in touch with his family. He was especially anxious to know what had become of his daughter. One day he came into the office, very much excited, having in his hand a newspaper. He shouted, 'I believe I have found my daughter.' He held up the paper and said, 'Here is a list of the nurses who are training in one of the hospitals, and one of those nurses has the same name as my daughter.' He said, 'Will you get in touch with her immediately?'

143

Helms agreed, of course, but warned him that it might be possible that she was someone else with the same name. Then he turned to Helms and said, 'Mr. Helms, what have we been praying for? Will you get in touch with the hospital?' The man's faith surprised Helms, so he got in touch with the hospital right away, and spoke to the nurse. She said, 'Yes, no doubt he is my father. My mother has passed away, but if father is there and doing right, I will be glad to come and meet him.' So they made an arrangement for father and daughter to meet, and what better place could they find than the front room of this 'House of Peace' in Osborn Place? Daughter and father were joined together again and they kept in touch with each other until the father passed away."

The two houses that remained in Osborn Place were the first Goodwill Industries workshops in America. Eventually, the city changed the name of Osborn Place to Helms Place. Helms also built The Church of All Nations on a part of the land where these houses stood.

The spirit in which Edgar Helms built the foundation of Goodwill Industries embodied his belief that everyone should be his brother's keeper. It was not enough that he should offer training and jobs for persons who wished to work, but through his dynamic belief in the power of goodness and goodwill, Helms touched lives wherever he found them.

In his book *The Redemption of the South End* (1915) by E.C.E. Dorion, the author visited the industrial plant at Morgan Memorial. His reaction to the work center:

"The variety of the work carried on at the Morgan will surprise any person who will take the trouble to

The Church of All Nations sign was a beacon to the crowds that came to Morgan Memorial Goodwill Industries each day. (From "The House of Goodwill," Morgan Memorial Press, 1925).

visit the institution," Dorion wrote. 'I never thought you had anything so extensive as this,' is the expression that drops from the lips of person after person as he goes from floor to floor of the six-story building.' "

Dorion's work is the story of the founding and building of Morgan Chapel by its founder, Henry Morgan, and the work continued there by Edgar Helms. In his book Dorion describes the vitality of life at the work center of Morgan Memorial in detail. "One who visits this part of the Morgan will be genuinely surprised, and pleased also, as he sees this modern development in relief work. It is rich tonic. In one room to be seen are the carpenters at work. We must remember that all of these men have been picked up from the street, or have come in, broken in spirit, or have been reached through the revival services. They take a broken chair, for instance, and make a new leg for it. It is then sanded, touched up, given a new rung, or anything else that is needed, painted and behold! You have a new chair. Does it require much imagination to see the possibilities of this department in turning out the products of the store and giving honest, remunerative employment to the unfortunate?"

The conditions of Boston's South End in the first decade of the new century proclaimed the need of relief work for those who had disabilities or could not find work. Helms' work center at Morgan Memorial employed both men and women, even giving

The early Goodwill Industries helped many destitute men overcome alcoholism and poverty in the Fred H. Seavey Settlement. (Photo from Morgan Memorial Goodwill Industries, Inc.).

employment to older children who needed to support their families. Dorion describes the relief he saw when visiting Morgan Memorial.

"It is in these departments, divided and subdivided to meet the requirements of the work, and in the printing office, the store, and other parts of the building, that these broken-down men and women and unfortunates of society who are battling with the world, are given a chance. One can hardly conceive of the far-reaching effects that such an opportunity may have. Some will become skillful if they are kept for a while; others will be tided over a hard spot; all will be given courage and help in asserting their self-respect. For when a man works for his bread, he can hold his head erect. This industry may be charity because it is conceived in a spirit of helpfulness, and not in that of mere money-making, but it is a charity that has about it no tinge of pauperism."

Helms' concept of selling the mended goods and clothing in stores at the Morgan and initial branch stores in South Boston, East Cambridge, Roxbury Crossing and Charlestown completed the most unique service to the community of its day. Dorion wrote in 1913: "The product of the industry is then sold for what it is worth. How much that means to the poor in these times of high prices! A fair price – but it is a price, and here again self-respect is saved, and pauperism is eliminated. It would be almost

The early Goodwill Industries taught workers to refurbish and repair donations such as shoes.

impossible to exaggerate the importance of such an institution."

Dorion wrote of an experience that he witnessed as he toured the store at Morgan Memorial. "One day, a fine looking man walked in and asked the privilege of a confidential talk. He was a floorwalker in a large department store of the city. He had had a hard time – sickness, reverses, and trouble – and had been unable to buy the clothes that needed. Finally they told him at the store that he must either get a new suit of clothes or leave; but he could not afford to buy one. When he went out of the Morgan he had a new suit, and he had made arrangements to pay for it gradually. The Morgan store had come to his rescue by having in stock what he needed at a price within his reach. If the pragmatic test were applied to this phase of the institution, then it is certainly a success, for it works. And a success it is! This is the seal that must be placed on this unique phase of the work at Morgan Memorial."

Another testimony to the strength of his resolve and to the workers who served him and his ideals came shortly after Helms created the first workshop in Osborn Place.

Many of the women that Helms employed to mend clothing had small children and they could not leave them at home, nor did they have the money to secure sitters to care for their children. There happened to be a young woman who had become interested in the services that Helms was providing at Morgan Chapel and when she heard Helms speaking of the difficulty of the problem that these women had, she came forward to speak to him.

"I love children," she said softly, "and have much experience caring for them. I have been a nurse for the rich children of the Back Bay and suburbs. I shall be glad to come and take care of these children

The philosophy of Goodwill Industries has remained steadfast over the past century – provide real-world job skills so people can become self-sufficient members of their communities. (A welder at Morgan Memorial Goodwill Industries, Boston. Photo from Morgan Memorial Goodwill Industries, Inc.).

while the mothers are at work." Helms studied her face and saw her sincerity, but answered politely, "Why would you give up your prosperous job and take charge of the poor babies around our Chapel?" The woman burst into tears and confessed to the pastor that she had always prayed that she might sometime have poor children to care for. Persuaded by her sincere demeanor Helms asked her wages would she demand, to which she replied, "Give me a place to sleep and something to eat and that will be enough." Still Helms wished to impress upon her the gravity of their need at Morgan Chapel and answered, "We have no bed or cribs." To which the woman replied, "You can use the old settees down in the basement. There are cushions on those settees, and I can manage for a while to take care of the children in this way."

Thus started one of the first employment day nurseries in the city of Boston, and for the next thirty years Miss Mary Fagan took care of hundreds of children while the mothers worked. The work of Mary Fagan and scores of similarly dedicated workers formed the first Goodwill Industries at Morgan Chapel. Helms would say of Mary Fagan, "During the thirty years she has been with Morgan Memorial, about three thousand different babies have been warmed with the glow of her motherly heart. If she ever showed partiality, it was always in behalf of the neediest and most ill-favored."

The influence of workers such as Mary Fagan and another children's worker, Kate F. Hobart, touched the lives of so many. Moore recalled one such story:

"One day a few years ago a fine, splendid looking young man came to the office and asked if Miss Fagan was still living. We were sorry to have to report to him that Miss Fagan had passed on. 'Well,' he said, 'Is Miss Hobart here?' We were glad to tell him that Miss Hobart was indeed still with us. Then he told us his story:

"Years ago because of the sickness of my father, we were forced down and lived on Ohio Street right opposite your institution. On account of my father's illness my mother had to work, and so my sisters and I were put in your Day Nursery. We shall never forget the kindness shown us by Miss Fagan and, also, of the opportunity it was for us to be taken care of so well while mother worked in one of your workshops. Then later you found a position for her outside.'

"My father was tubercular and some of my friends rallied round and raised sufficient money for us to go out on the coast. Father lived only three years afterward and, also, mother passed on. We managed somehow to finish our education up through high school. Then sister and I opened a small store. I am glad to say that we have prospered.'

"I am visiting Boston for the first time since we left. Coming in on the train, I kept looking for the Morgan Memorial building. Then I saw it. I determined that my first call should be here at Morgan Memorial.'

"After the man had left, I saw Miss Hobart later and shared with her the generous check he had left us to carry on our children's work. Attached to the check was written a note: *Cast thy bread upon the waters, and it will return after many days.*"

Helms called Kate Hobart "the most unselfish worker he had ever known," adding that "She has served longer than any other worker at Morgan Memorial, and worked for years with no pay at all." When asked about the loyalty of his staff, Helms would often tear up. When asked later in his life about the service of Hobart to Morgan Memorial, Helms said, "Some folks are born saints; others are made saints by many testings and trials. Saint Kate belongs to both kinds. No matter how trying her own burden, she has learned to bear it by lifting the burdens of others."

It soon became apparent that the old buildings in Osborn Place were altogether too small for the expanding industrial work that employed scores of workers. Helms and his staff had created woodwork, furniture repair and upholstery, appliance repair, the mending of clothing and shoe repair. His industrial work encompassed many services, and more were employed. Through a good friend, Helms met Adolphus Lindfield, a Methodist minister in New Hampshire who had two prominent parishioners, George and John Henry, who were

While a teacher in Boston, Kate F. Hobart worked for free at Morgan Memorial Goodwill Industries. Upon her death, she left Morgan Memorial one of its first endowments, $3,000 to be used for children's work. (Photo from Morgan Memorial Goodwill Industries, Inc.).

brothers. The Henrys owned manufacturing plants and through the church had become acquainted with the work of Edgar Helms in Boston. Helms made a call on them and secured funding to build three new buildings to house industrial activities at Morgan Memorial. In total, the Henry brothers gave Helms over $350,000. While the expansion into the Osborn Place had seemed large, this expansion was immense and provided Helms the room he needed to dramatically grow the relief services he had started. In addition to the new buildings, the Henry brothers were so impressed with the work of Helms, over the years they helped fund an enlargement of the Children's Settlement, the Seminary Settlement for Lost Men, and the Eliza A. Henry Settlement for Elderly Women.

Helms applied for, and received, a charter from the state of Massachusetts to form the "National Cooperative Industrial Relief Association" to promote the concepts developed at Morgan Memorial which could be used for other similar efforts throughout the United States.

Helms wrote in his memoirs that the "principles underlying Goodwill Industries are often overlooked:

"Not charity but a chance."
"Saving the waste of men and things."
"The best help is the help that helps
one to help himself by helping someone else."

The expanded Morgan Memorial Goodwill Industries included the industrial plant where employees restored collected items, learning trades and skills as they worked. (Photo from Morgan Memorial Goodwill Industries, Inc.)

These slogans reveal both the method and spirit of Goodwill Industries as Helms and his early staff envisioned them. His concepts were revolutionary.

Goodwill Industries took discarded items donated by the public and employed men and women in need to bring both things and persons back to usefulness and well being. The renovated product entered upon a new career of service as a repaired, renovated or newly mended article. These things were then sold for a low price to people in need or who could not afford to buy new things, and the money was used to pay self-respecting wages to those who work.

Following the development of Goodwill Industries, the succeeding years added recognition and stability to the program. In 1918, leaders of the Methodist Church found in the Goodwill program a form of service they desired to sponsor in a number of cities. Upon conclusion of the Methodist Centenary Campaign, sufficient resources were provided so that Goodwill Industries could be established in thirty-five cities in the United States. To ensure administration and supervision of the new units to be started, the church organized the Bureau of Goodwill Industries in the Board of Missions of the Methodist Church. As its first superintendent, the Board of Missions invited Edgar Helms to serve. For a number of years, Helms provided leadership in the expansion and development of the program.

A place was identified for the Bureau in the Discipline of the Methodist Episcopal Church at the General Conference at Des Moines, 1920, and revised at the Kansas City General Conference, 1928.

With Helms as the driving force, Goodwill Industries gradually spread across the United States, offering programs to help the "unemployables" enter the work force. As more Goodwill agencies were created, a parent organization of the membership of Goodwills was created for administrative purposes. The first body was called Goodwill Industries of America, Inc. By 1926, Helms was touring the world telling the story of Goodwill Industries and laying the groundwork for an international movement. When the Great Depression caused mass unemployment, Goodwill narrowed the focus of its services to people with disabilities.

Helms wrote "I would be well if those who are trying to lift the world out of our present economic slump would study the workings of Goodwill Industries. It is saving the waste of things. It is salvaging cast-off materials and, in the process, is paying self-respecting wages to thousands who have been thrown on the industrial scrap-heap."

In the manual that Helms offered as a blueprint for Goodwill Industries start-ups and policies, printed in 1932, Helms added, "The Goodwill Industries is organized to save material waste and turn it into human well-being." Helms saw that little, if anything, should to be wasted. He spearheaded a worldwide movement on the discards of others. He pioneered rural Goodwill Industries as well as urban ones, using the former for recreation camps for underprivileged children and the elderly and sick.

Edgar Helms likened his movement to the mission of the church itself, "Gathering up the fragments that remain that nothing be lost. To save lost, wasted lives was the passion of our Lord. Surely Goodwill Industries have no apologies to make while following Him."

From the time that Dr. Helms started his work in Boston, he found that all kinds of nationalities were living in his part of the city. To accommodate this diverse population, Helms conceived of a church for all nationalities. Praying fervently for guidance, Helms received a call within a few short weeks from a Unitarian church that was to be taken down. The minister asked Helms if he could use the beautiful brown stone that was used as a façade for the church. While Helms was not ready to build his Church of All Nations, he readily agreed to take the stone and within two years, the beautiful Church of All Nations had been built and was attached to the Morgan Memorial Chapel. As was customary of Helms, the church was fully paid for before construction was completed. Helms called his church a "Fellowship. A place where goodwill and love are regarded paramount to creed."

In addition to the Church of All Nations, Helms had successfully built the day nursery and Children's Settlement in South Athol, Massachusetts, and a Men's Camp near the Children's Day Nursery where "men could escape the harshness of the city." It was named the Fred H. Seavey Seminary

Settlement. He had a successful settlement operation in Boston's North End as well, where the concepts of Goodwill Industries were tried and perfected. Within a few years Helms founded the Eliza A. Henry Home for Women. On the South Athol property, Helms also began a large Fresh Air Farm and an Industrial Plantation.

Edgar Helms believed in the sanctity of Goodwill Industries. He wished for it always to be tied to a religious atmosphere. As subsequent Goodwill agencies began in other cities across America, Helms insisted that all should have morning chapel services. He felt that men and women should receive not just job training and assistance in finding a job, but spiritual guidance, personal and family counseling if needed, all adding up to a total commitment for an individual in the program. While Goodwill Industries was created for the disadvantaged, it quickly focused on the needs of the handicapped and disabled population in cities across the country. Helms was particularly interested in saving waste. He was fond of the saying: "Goodwill Industries saves the waste in men and things."

Goodwill Industries of Boston began in 1902, although the name 'Goodwill Industries' would not be coined until a few years later in Brooklyn, New York. The charter was granted August 29, 1905, and the name adopted was "The Morgan Memorial Cooperative Industries and Stores, Inc. Dr. Francis H. Slack, one of the founding members and early

161

workers in the program, was named the first president. For over twenty years, Dr. Slack served diligently until his death in 1932. Mr. William Kurth, a Boston attorney, was elected president and served for more than twenty years as well. The third president of Goodwill Industries of America, Inc. was James T. Buckley, president of the Philco Corporation in Philadelphia.

The first Goodwill Industries agency to form outside of Boston was in Brooklyn, New York, in 1915. Of paramount importance to the founding of Goodwill Industries agencies in other cities was Oliver A. Friedman, who served as executive secretary of the National Association of Goodwill Industries and Bureau of Goodwill Industries. Together with Helms, Friedman traveled all over the country consulting and planning with persons who had become interested in the Goodwill movement. Friedman would later become secretary of the Cleveland Goodwill Industries. Later, Percy J. Trevethan, who had worked for twenty years at the Morgan Memorial, became the executive secretary of the national movement and succeeded, after Helms' death, in establishing a number of other Goodwill Industries. Trevethan moved the national office to the Washington, D.C. area, where it has been housed until the present, now in Bethesda, MD.

During the next twenty years, Helms and his staff organized ninety-five independent Goodwill agencies.

City	Organized
Morgan Chapel, Boston	1902
Brooklyn, New York	1915
San Francisco, California	1916
St. Louis, Missouri	1916
Los Angeles, California	1917
Cincinnati, Ohio	1917
Baltimore, Maryland	1917
Cleveland, Ohio	1918
Denver, Colorado	1918
Duluth, Minnesota	1919
Jersey City, New Jersey	1919
Pittsburgh, Pennsylvania	1919
Philadelphia, Pennsylvania	1919
Milwaukee, Wisconsin	1919
St. Paul, Minnesota	1919
Chicago, Illinois	1920
Buffalo, New York	1920
Tacoma, Washington	1920
Lowell, Massachusetts	1920
Wilmington, Delaware	1921
Detroit, Michigan	1921
New York City, New York	1922
Nashville, Tennessee	1922
Chattanooga, Tennessee	1922
Seattle, Washington	1923
Louisville, Kentucky	1923
Lynn, Massachusetts	1923
Sioux City, Iowa	1924
Minneapolis, Minnesota	1924

Grand Junction, Colorado	1924
Youngstown, Ohio	1924
Atlanta, Georgia	1925
Kansas City, Missouri	1925
Norfolk, Virginia	1925
Santa Ana, California	1925
West Tulsa, Oklahoma	1925
Springfield, Massachusetts	1926
Portland, Oregon	1926
Winston-Salem, North Carolina	1926
Shreveport, Louisiana	1926
Norwalk, Connecticut	1926
Tokyo, Japan	1926
San Jose, California	1926
Shanghai, China	1926
Springfield, Illinois	1926
Philippine Islands	1926
Akron, Ohio	1927
Mexico City, Mexico	1927
Aberdeen, Washington	1927
Brisbane, Australia	1927
Colombo, Ceylon	1927
Calcutta, India	1927
Sidney, Australia	1927
Melbourne, Australia	1927
Adelaide, Australia	1927
Perth, Australia	1927
Terre Haute, Indiana	1927
Zanesville, Ohio	1927
Santa Cruz, California	1927

Nashua, New Hampshire	1927
Canton, Ohio	1928
Dallas, Texas	1928
Birmingham, Alabama	1928
Little Rock, Arkansas	1928
Lorain, Ohio	1928
Troy, New York	1928
East St. Louis, Missouri	1928
San Bernardino, California	1928
Mohawk Trail, Massachusetts	1928
Indianapolis, Indiana	1929
Montevideo, Uruguay	1929
Long Beach, California	1929
Hammond & Calumet District, Indiana	1929
San Diego, California	1930
Pueblo, Colorado	1930
Jacksonville, Florida	1930
Winnipeg, Canada	1930
Lexington, Kentucky	1930
New Haven, Connecticut	1930
Decatur, Illinois	1930
Roanoke, Virginia	1931
Springfield, Illinois	1931
New Albany, Indiana	1931
Saginaw, Michigan	1931
Granite City, Illinois	1932
Ottawa, Ontario, Canada	1932
Alton, Illinois	1932
Flint, Michigan	1932
Oslo, Norway	1932

Lincoln, Nebraska	1932
Lawrence & Merrimack Valley	1932
Portland, Maine	1933
Peoria, Illinois	1933
Richmond, Virginia	1933
St. Joseph, Missouri	1933
Oakland, California	1933
Biddeford, Maine	1933
Omaha, Nebraska	1933
Toledo, Ohio	1933
Sacramento, California	1933
Dayton, Ohio	1934
Portsmouth, New Hampshire	1934
Sarnia, Ontario, Canada	1934

Everywhere he went, Edgar Helms inspired and preached his philosophy. "The Goodwill Industries stands at the very bottom of the industrial ladder," Helms was proud to proclaim. "It gives opportunity to those broken by all kinds of misfortunes. Not by condescending snobbiness, but by brotherly cooperation it seeks to rebuild the lives and fortunes of the neediest."

To the eager businessmen and women who listened to Helms as he traveled from city to city inspiring others to form Goodwill agencies, Helms closed almost every presentation with the same warning. "It would be an unspeakable calamity, a repudiation of our heavenly mission if the Goodwill Industries failed in its spiritual ministry. Why employ a responsible worker who does not radiate love and goodwill? How can one who does not pray, teach others to pray? What is the example of a worker in a responsible position who neglects the Goodwill Chapel services?" Helms encouraged civic leaders to work with spiritual, industrial and educational leaders to form partnerships and alliances to serve more people, reaching out with the hand of goodwill.

In 1932, writing the introduction of the Goodwill Manual of Operations, Helms stressed the need to support the disabled. "The Goodwill program," he wrote, "must give more and more intelligent and sympathetic consideration to the training and employment of the handicapped. This means the employment of competent overseers who are able to teach. It also means that such Goodwills must adopt an equitable piece system of wages. There must be a proper subsidy provided for more expensive supervision, because the Goodwill Industries must take on more than ever the work of those technical schools, which would not accept such old and backward scholars. Here is perhaps one of the best fields in which Goodwill Industries can be employed."

Helms' vision set an early course toward what is now a 1.9-billion-dollar nonprofit organization. Today, Goodwill Industries International is the world's largest private-sector employer of people with disabilities and disadvantaged conditions. Helms' concept of providing "a chance, not charity," has expanded into 187 autonomous members in the U.S.

and Canada, and 54 associate members in 37 countries outside of North America. His vision has helped several million people recognize and fill their individual roles in society and the workplace.

Now in the centennial year, 2002, of Goodwill Industries, new horizons have been set for the movement. At this time in history it is more than fitting to quote Frederick Moore, who recorded the progress of Goodwill Industries for the first fifty years in his book *The Golden Threads of Destiny*. His chronology of the first fifty years gives greater importance to centennial initiatives of Goodwill Industries' first one hundred years. In his book Moore writes:

"Now at the midpoint of a century of service we look to the past for the assurance of the future. The record of these fifty years – more than three hundred thousand persons served and more than one hundred sixty millions of dollars in self-respecting wages paid – is the foundation upon which we seek to serve the need of the present and future years. That which has been accomplished through love, cooperation and Goodwill is only a forecast of the measure of opportunity of service the future holds. The heritage of the years and the spirit of the founders are present-day incentives to larger goals of achievement.

"During the first half-century of service Goodwill Industries has made significant progress. Each year these 101 units serve nearly 25,000 handicapped and disabled persons. But this is only a beginning. Figures available from the United States Office of Vocational Rehabilitation of the Federal Security Agency tell us that at any given moment there are at least 250,000 persons who need the rehabilitative services of Goodwill Industries. A still large number – estimated to be nearly eight million – of our citizens are handicapped."

At the funeral of Edgar J. Helms, on December 27, 1942, Bishop G. Bromley Oxnam of the Methodist Church summarized the contribution made by Helms in this way:

"He knew that men must be born again. He was not only for changed men, but also for changed communities and changed nations. His message was personal, and social. He may have studied church history when in Europe on that fellowship, but he also studied cooperatives. He returned to give himself to Boston, to the nation, and finally through his church to the world.

"In Dr. Helms' concept, Goodwill Industries was not run for profit, but for service. They translated the command of the Master, 'Thou shalt love thy neighbor as thyself.' Helms believed that there should be work for everybody and everybody should work. Helms said that "Goodwill exists for 'service' and not for 'profit.' There are no 'profits' in Goodwill Industries. All earnings go to the workers according to their need and ability after the expenses for maintenance of the plant and necessary overhead are paid.

"Dr. Helms believed that Goodwill Industries should be managed by a democracy, 'more democratic than the dreams of any social agitator.' He held firm that workers should have representation on the Board of Directors. 'Every responsible worker,' Helms wrote, 'realizes that he can only work for himself successfully in so far as he improves the wellbeing of others. If he fails in blessing others, he is a failure in Goodwill Industries.' Workers must 'communicate the spirit of service to every one employed with him. It is all for each and each for all without discrimination as to color, creed or character.' Dr. Helms held donors and shoppers in high regard, saying, 'Purchasers in our stores are contributors to the work of serving others quite as essentially as those who give necessary capital for buildings and equipment, or who contribute materials on which the workers labor.' "

E.C.E. Dorion wrote of Helms: "Perhaps one of the most outstanding characteristics of Edgar J. Helms is his thorough faith in man. There are plenty of people who have faith in God, but to have his faith in man, especially man in the slums, man who has marred the divine image almost beyond recognition, who has wallowed in the mire, and made a veritable beast of himself – that is different. But unlike most in the church, Helms sees the divine image in even the lowest sinner, and he believes in the goodness there to be found when touched by the grace of God. He sees men redeemed and restored to self-respecting lives."

Late in his life, Edgar Helms would write, "Persons who know my home and upbringing can readily understand how I naturally became a Goodwill Industries founder and promoter. I was nearly a grown man before I wore other clothes than those my dear, thrifty Yankee mother made for me

A 50th anniversary commemorative painting of Edgar J. Helms and the original Morgan Memorial Chapel.

from my father's well-worn suits. The first suit I remember having was one I earned from trapping muskrats in Iowa. I was brought up to save – yet, so far I as know I have never been called stingy. I have been accused of almost everything else. I have rejoiced in saving for others and sharing with them. It is a great joy to make others rich – especially if we can enrich the poor and unfortunate. I am really getting a 'kick' out of life as I think from time to time that thousands of folks are receiving millions of dollars that Goodwill Industries saved from being waste. If any rich man on earth is getting more fun out of his family and his job than I am, he is welcome to it. All the real estate I own on earth is a half interest in half a burial lot in the cemetery in Eagle Grove, Iowa. It is enough for me."

In his memoirs, Helms wrote, "The world could become a paradise in a few generations if government, science and industry would make 'service' their chief objective and no longer exploit others, but build up a better race of human beings. The unlimited resources of the world could be utilized in making all parts of the world useful and beautiful. If every man loved our Father God and his neighbor as himself, all men would walk the earth as sons of God and there would be a new race, where the excellencies of all would become the possession of each. There would be no poor – not even poor sinners, in that universe of love and goodwill. Even religious controversy, rivalry and prejudice would dissolve in a love that serves everyone and seeks not her own. The Kingdom of God would indeed be at hand and the world could be evangelized in one generation if business, politics, education and religion were converted and born again to the Gospel of Service in the Spirit of Goodwill."

Goodwill in the 21st Century
A Century of Growth

For over two hundred million households, Goodwill has become a household word for recycling unwanted items. From burlap bags to collection centers around the world, Goodwill Industries has prospered and grown.

Goodwill has played important roles in times of recession and prosperity and was instrumental during World War II in serving as a collection system for scarce war materials. Following the war, Goodwill retrained thousands of men and women with disabilities sustained in combat. That effort continued during the conflicts in Korea and later in Vietnam.

Governmental agencies such as state offices of Vocational Rehabilitation have counted on their unique partnerships with Goodwill to provide job training and employment assistance to over 2.5 million disabled Americans. During the important legislation in the 1990s to transition millions of Americans from welfare rolls to self-sufficiency, it was Goodwill Industries that the government chose as a key partner to support their difficult, yet important initiatives. The results have been impressive and successful. What began as a way to reduce the flow of federal dollars to the impoverished has resulted in self-sufficiency and self-respect for millions of individuals and families.

There is much work to be done, however. Worldwide, over three billion people are looking for work or are not making enough money to rise out of poverty. Over 350 million people of working age worldwide have disabilities. Unemployment statistics in some countries for the disabled is as high as 80%. In the United States, 67% of people with disabilities who want to work are unemployed.

Poverty rates for the United States and Canada are still high. In the U.S., 11.3% of the population, over 30 million individuals are impoverished. In Canada it is even higher at 16.2%.

Although welfare-to-work initiatives have been partially successful, only 10% of families that leave the welfare rolls for work are earning enough to be considered self-sufficient.

Much more work is needed to be done throughout the world. Goodwill leadership has set a goal to directly serve twenty million persons in the next eighteen years, by the year 2020.

This vision grew from grass-roots meetings across the country as each Goodwill agency staff looked at ways of expanding services to more and more of its community citizens. The commitment has been coined as the "Goodwill Industries 21st Century Initiative" by Goodwill Industries International president George Kessinger, the national Goodwill staff and executives from member organizations.

The combined vision statement of Goodwill Industries as it begins its second hundred years as a movement reads:

The people of Goodwill Industries believe in the power of work to transform lives. Work is central to economic self-sufficiency and the ability to support one's family. The community is a better place when its citizens are able to work and contribute to the community's strength and success. We believe that all work has dignity, and work adds to the dignity of individuals and their families. Goodwill Industries' vision is a world where people are able to be productive workers regardless of disability or previous work history. Everyone will have the resources to learn work skills according to one's aptitude and the needs of employers. These resources will include those that are central to the job itself, as well as those that support employment, such as transportation, family care or health.

Edgar Helms could have written the vision statement himself at the turn of the last century. He and his early workers believed "in the power of work to transform lives" rather than in the concept of charity or welfare dollars that would not lead to self-sufficiency. Helms clearly saw the dignity that hard work brought to wage earners and their families; dignity that touched the deepest need in people, offering people a "hand up, rather than a hand out."

The vision statement of the Goodwill Industries 21st Century Initiative reflects the core belief that all people, regardless of disability or disadvantage, have the right to work, whatever their work history or severity of their disability or impoverishment. As Edgar Helms preached to the "poor in spirit" on the street corner in front of Murphy's Tavern in Boston, so does the vision of Goodwill Industries speak to individuals today. Helms said, "Never has the need been greater," and the same could be said of conditions in 2002, as they were in 1902.

The collective visions of leaders of Goodwill in 2002 states that "Everyone will have the resources to learn work skills according to one's aptitude." This states clearly that everyone has the right to work and self-sufficiency, even if the tasks of some may not measure up to the tasks of others. The spirit of the Goodwill founder is alive and well in such a statement. Edgar Helms never quantified the amount of work a person accomplished as the measure of that person's success, only the fact that they had the right and opportunity to work.

The circle of influence of Goodwill Industries continues to grow. From the first city blocks surrounding the Morgan Chapel in Boston, the breadth of Goodwill's influence is now worldwide. From the first workers who came to the industrial work center in Boston, Goodwill has continually found innovative ways to reach anyone in need, and anyone who has the desire to improve their life through work. The methods of sewing a patch on a pair of worn pants, or of sanding and repainting a scratched piece of furniture have changed to reaching thousands at a time through on-line computer tutorials in the privacy of the worker's home. The methods have changed but not the philosophy.

Twenty Million by 2020

Having served over five million individuals in its first hundred years as a movement, Goodwill staff and volunteers began to formulate a new goal as the Centennial year of Goodwill's history approached. The new vision was not monetary. It went to the core philosophy of Edgar Helms' belief that the member organization must first serve people. Twenty million by 2020 became the vision. It became a rallying point for centennial celebrations held throughout 2002, as the movement turned one hundred years old.

To accomplish such an impressive vision in a relatively short time period of only eighteen years, several strategies were developed.

The new initiative simply gave direction to this lofty goal. The work of Goodwill Industries would not waver from the same work it had been accomplishing around the world for the first hundred years. The commitment of Edgar Helms to serve people, simply for the love of people, is firmly intact within the movement.

Prepare More Persons With Special Needs

It is the work of Goodwill Industries to increase the economic self-sufficiency of people with disabilities and others who experience barriers to employment. With new and wider reaching training methods, such as through use of the Internet, Goodwill's vision continues to provide, directly or in alliance with others, education and training services, work experience opportunities, and other services that create opportunities for employment, or that alleviate or remove barriers to employment.

As the global economy ebbs and flows, Goodwill firmly believes that the unemployed need to be served first, as well as those who are working but need to improve their skills or learn new skills, so they might move closer to their goal of self-sufficiency. A "hand up, not a hand out" rings as true in the 21st century as it did at the dawn of the 20th century. The needs of mankind are not served permanently through charity. It is only through work that a man or woman can care for themselves and their family. It is only through work that a person's dignity can be restored.

Goodwill Industries is committed to widening its sphere of influence by serving more youths who lack vocational direction to develop their skills and values they need to be productive and to become contributing members of society. While the value of

179

educating young minds is certainly of paramount importance, Goodwill believes that teaching work values, while obtaining valuable job-related skills training is equally valuable as a young boy or girl approaches his/her working years. Workforce productivity in an intrinsically learned behavior, Goodwill believes, and is continually fed by the desire to be self-sufficient. That strong desire is alive and well in the minds of 21st century young people as they enter the workforce and share in the collective dreams of all workers.

For those who are working, Goodwill believes it must provide opportunities, directly, or in partnership with others, for continued education and training so individuals can keep pace in a changing workforce. Each decade seems to bring new challenges to the workforce as some skills are needed less while others are in greater demand. That concept is certainly true in the information explosion of the present. The age of computer revolutionized communications technology has brought an end to some jobs while creating others. Teaching job skills to individuals is necessary so they may make those adjustments in the changing workforce is the goal of Goodwill, and a vital part of its 21st Century Initiative.

Embracing The Family

It is the vision of Goodwill Industries to help find or provide the necessary resources that support employment for the family. While the physical makeup the of the family might look different in the year 2002, Goodwill Industries recognizes that serving a family, be it one, two or more workers in the unit, is often vital to the family's success at becoming self-sufficient.

The goal of Goodwill in the years to come is to find and help provide family needs such as transportation, health care, child care, adult care and other issues related to the family unit so workers can stay on the job and be more productive. In the founding years of Goodwill Industries, Edgar Helms recognized that childcare was a major issue in keeping many workers productive. It is no less of an issue today. The cost of childcare is a financial strain on families and adds a significant barrier to many that seek employment or additional job training skills.

Transportation is another vital component to successful employment. In major cities, mass transit provides opportunities for many workers to get to and from work, but even in large communities, bus lines do not always extend to new work environments. In smaller cities the problem is exacerbated where public transportation might not exist at all. Many Goodwill agencies have developed in-house transportation services providing donated automobiles to those in need so they may get or keep a job. The gap between minimum wage positions and being able to afford an automobile is often insurmountable. The path to self-sufficiency is not always about working alone when the worker is miles from his or her place of employment with no affordable or reliable way to get to and from that place.

As employers seek to blaze the path of providing livable salary and benefits to their employees, health care and health insurance issues are becoming more and more 21st century issues. Goodwill Industries recognizes that it needs to support and provide health care strategies and solutions to support family health so workers can stay on the job and remain productive in the workplace. Health care concerns and solutions for working families are broad and varied, but Goodwill recognizes that it must position itself to be able to provide and seek answers to these health-related workforce issues.

Childcare was provided to workers early in the history of Goodwill's workplace. Helms recognized the need to assist workers by providing skilled nursery and childcare workers and activities. Through the years of the industrial and technological revolutions, however, childcare issues have grown further from the workplace rather than closer. This barrier to gainful employment or job training for better employment has left many families behind.

Goodwill recognizes that it must seek successful strategies and support systems to provide childcare as well as adult care for family members of workers if the family is to succeed in its goal of self-sufficiency.

Goodwill Industries has recognized and supported the family structure since its formation. It also recognizes that dealing effectively with family issues is central to the workforce capabilities of the family and therefore, dedicates itself to providing solutions to as many family issues as possible to be in support of the workers within the family.

Develop Mission-Enhancing Business Opportunities

Because of its unique position in communities throughout the world, and because of its rich and successful one-hundred-year history, Goodwill Industries believes it can continue to partner effectively with business by collectively leveraging its resources. While the goal is jobs for disabled and disadvantaged workers, Goodwill believes in and is dedicated to creating opportunities for their target populations to develop mutually beneficial alliances with businesses, government and non-governmental organizations. These alliances would support the mission of Goodwill to provide jobs for workers, particularly disabled and disadvantaged individuals.

As many companies expand their sphere of influence outside the borders of their home country, globalization issues within those companies might have far-reaching effect for a member organization such as Goodwill. By leveraging resources from one community and agency to another, Goodwill believes it can find hidden or untapped resources for its unique population. In the poorest regions of the world, Goodwill seeks to develop micro-enterprising programs to enhance its position. The international organization of Goodwill Industries also seeks to expand its physical presence in nations where environmental conditions or war have severely crippled the workforce and local economies.

From its inception, the independent agencies of Goodwill Industries have formed unique alliances with government and non-governmental groups to serve those with disabilities or disadvantages. By strengthening partnerships with local government and business, Goodwill believes it can more effectively serve individuals in this manner than by acting alone. Aligning itself with other businesses to support its mission of job readiness and job placement remains the steadfast objective of the movement.

Technology Training

Expanding technology has revolutionized the workplace. It has also created a technology divide in the population that has left millions of workers feeling inadequate or unable to be productive.

Goodwill believes it must include appropriate technology training in its broad curriculum base to assist those workers and bridge that divide. By identifying emerging technologies that increase productivity among workers, training within Goodwill agencies will continue to be effective for workers and employers alike.

The technology divide is as much economic as it is educational. Not everyone can afford home computers or technological devices needed to become adequately prepared to be productive in the workplace. Goodwill Industries recognizes that it must assist workers everywhere, but particularly disabled and disadvantaged workers, by providing access to the equipment and knowledge of how to effectively use it.

Optimize Goodwill Resources

One hundred years of Goodwill activity throughout the world has created a wealth of resources. Collectively, the agency believes it needs to pool resources, draw from its unique set of strengths and continue to build upon its assets while examining its weaknesses and inadequacies. As the organization grows throughout the world its members recognize that the old or existing governance and operating policies might need to be changed to meet the needs of a changing workplace. What seems of primary importance to the leadership of Goodwill is the mission and goal, not the policies and procedures. For every business, the need to change and adapt to human and market conditions is key to survival and success. One need only look at the rise and fall of previous global giants and how they did not change internally in a changing world to comprehend how fleeting success often can be.

While Goodwill Industries was founded on concepts of humility and service, it recognizes how easily the tremendous growth and success of its first one hundred years could alter those very principles and jeopardize its future. Goodwill leadership recognizes that to remain successful it must practice its own unique brand of continuing self-sufficiency. While being ever vigilant of market changes Goodwill Industries must not abandon its founding principles and must continue to be a good steward to its employees, partnerships and those to whom it serves.

The 21st Century Initiative requires all of Goodwill to expand its services and relationships dramatically to reach the goal of twenty million by the year 2020. The movement could rest on its laurels of services to five million individuals during its first century of service, but clearly, it is not resting. Setting the bar ever higher, Goodwill leadership is striving toward an ambitious goal to serve, grow and adapt to the needs of individuals who have always needed its services. In the words of its founder, over one hundred years ago: "Friends of Goodwill, be dissatisfied with your work until every handicapped and unfortunate person in your community has an opportunity to develop to his fullest usefulness and enjoy a maximum of abundant living."

References/Bibliography

Child & Adolescent Bipolar Foundation;
    www.bpkids.org
Differently Abled Winners Network;
    www.dawnser.home.mindspring.com/
Disabilities Studies and Services Center;
    www.dssc.org
eMedicine Journal, June 18, 2001, Vol. 2, No. 6;
    Congenital Cataracts; C Corina Gerontis,
    MD;www.eMedicine.com
Goodwill Industries International; www.goodwill.org
Goodwill Industries of Central North Carolina, Inc.;
    www.triadgoodwill.org
Kali Munro, M.Ed., Psychotherapist; *Incest and Child
    Sexual Abuse: Definitions, Perpetrators, Victims &
    Effects;* www.kalimunro.com
Kurshan, Nancy; *Women & Imprisonment in the U.S.,
    History & Current Reality;* www.prisonactivist.org
Morgan Memorial Goodwill Industries, Inc.
National Alliance for the Mentally Ill (NAMI);
    www.nami.org
National Depressive and Manic-Depressive Assn.;
    www.ndmda.org
National Institute of Neurological Disorders & Stroke;
    Cerebral Palsy: Hope Through Research;
    www.ninds.nih.gov.
National Institute on Drug Abuse; NIH Pub.#98-
    4327, Sept. 1998.
National Spinal Cord Injury Statistical Center
    (NSCISC); www.spinalcord.uab.edu
Office of Applied Studies; SAMHSA, National
    Household Survey on Drub Abuse, 1996.
Pioneering in Modern City Missions; Edgar J. Helms;
    Morgan Memorial Printing, 1927, Boston, MA.

References

Points of Light Foundation; www.pointsoflight.org

The Golden Threads of Destiny, Frederick C. Moore; Morgan Memorial Goodwill Press, Boston, MA., 1952.

The Goodwill Industries, A Manual; Morgan Memorial Goodwill Press, 1935, Boston, MA.

The Partially Sighted Society; www.rnib.org.uk

The Redemption of the South End, E.C.E. Dorion; Abingdon Press, New York, NY, 1915.

United Cerebral Palsy Associations, Inc; www.ucpa.org

U.S. Department of Justice, Office Justice Programs, Bureau of Justice Statistics; Survey of State Prison Inmates.

Women's Economic Agenda Project, May 1994.

Special thanks to: Theresa, Bernadette, Cynthia, Charles, Karan, Julios, Ed and Debbie for sharing their stories of perseverance.

Order Form

100 Years of Goodwill
Touching Lives Through the Power of Work

Please send _____ copies @ $14.95 each $_____

Shipping

$3.00 each book ($1 for each additional book) $_____
North Carolina residents please add 6% tax $_____
Canadian/Mexico residents add $2 for shipping $_____

Total $_____

Send order to:
Circe Press
(Publishers of Lifestyles Press)
P.O. Box 493
Greensboro, NC 27402
1-888-742-2155

Checks & Credit Cards payable to: Circe Press

Other in print titles by Steve Mundahl:

Beyond Betrayal
Driven to Succeed
There is Power in Belief